THE
PICTURE
ATLAS
OF THE WORLD

Illustrated by Brian Delf

DORLING KINDERSLEY
LONDON · NEW YORK · STUTTGART

A DORLING KINDERSLEY BOOK

Text by Richard Kemp

Art Editor Lester Cheeseman
Designer Marcus James
Project Editor Susan Peach
Senior Editor Emma Johnson
Consultant Keith Lye
Production Teresa Solomon
Art Director Roger Priddy

First published in Great Britain in 1991
by Dorling Kindersley Limited,
9 Henrietta Street, London WC2E 8PS

Reprinted (twice) with revisions 1991

A CIP catalogue record for this book is available from the British Library

ISBN 0-86318-599-1

Reproduced in Hong Kong by Bright Arts
Printed and bound in Italy by New Interlitho, Milan

CONTENTS

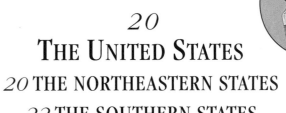

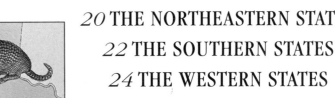

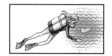

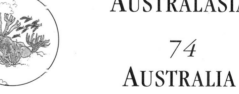
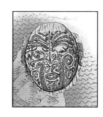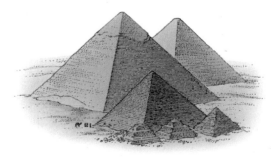

OUR PLANET EARTH

THE EARTH on which we live is one of a family of nine planets which circle around a star called the Sun. The Sun is just one of about 100,000 million stars in our galaxy. On a clear night you can see some of the other stars in the galaxy as a glow in the sky, called the Milky Way. Astronomers estimate that there may be as many as 10,000 million galaxies, which together make up the universe.

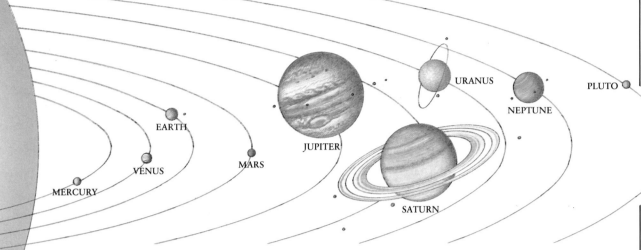

THE SOLAR SYSTEM

The Sun is much bigger than the planets. It has a diameter of about 1,392,000 km (864,948 miles). The diameter of the Earth at the Equator is only 12,714 km (7,747 miles).

The distance from the Sun to the Earth is about 150 million km (93 million miles). If a train left Earth at a speed of 175 kph (110 mph), it would take 96 years to reach the Sun.

THE ATMOSPHERE

The atmosphere is a layer of gases surrounding the Earth. It is about 1,000 km (621 miles) thick and is made of nitrogen, oxygen, carbon dioxide, water vapour, and small amounts of other gases. The atmosphere acts as a protective shield, absorbing much of the heat that reaches the Earth from the Sun. Without it, our whole planet would be burnt to a desert.

Most of the gases in the atmosphere are concentrated in the lowest part, which is called the troposphere. Above this is the stratosphere. This contains the ozone layer, which absorbs harmful ultra-violet rays from the Sun. Above the stratosphere are the mesosphere and the thermosphere. Here the gases are so thin that there is little difference between these parts of the atmosphere and space.

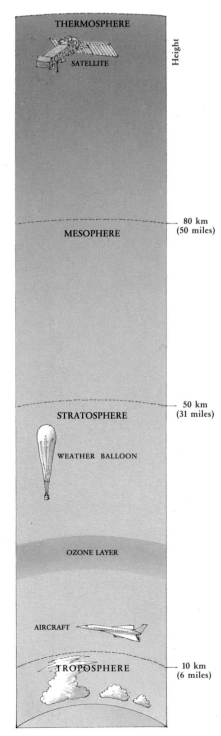

THE EARTH'S SHIELD

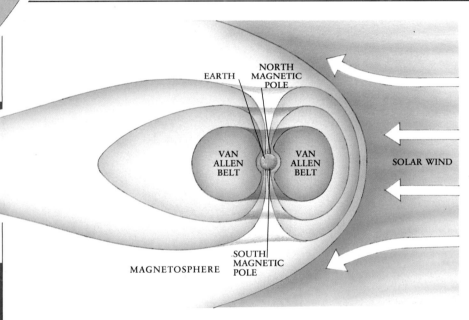

The Earth is like a giant magnet. It has two magnetic poles, which lie near the North and South Poles. The Earth's magnetism is probably caused by movement of the molten metals in its outer core. Around the Earth is a region called the magnetosphere, which acts as a huge shield. It protects the Earth from the solar wind, a stream of electrically charged particles from the Sun. Particles that get through the magnetosphere are trapped in the Van Allen belts.

THE SEASONS AND DAYS

It takes a year for the Earth to circle the Sun. The Earth is slightly tilted, so one half of the globe, or hemisphere, is closer to the Sun than the other. This tilt causes the seasons. The hemisphere tilted towards the Sun receives more heat, and so has summer, while the hemisphere that is tilted away has winter. As it circles the Sun, the Earth also spins on its axis, turning once every 24 hours. This rotation causes our days and nights. The side of the Earth facing the Sun has day, while the other side has night.

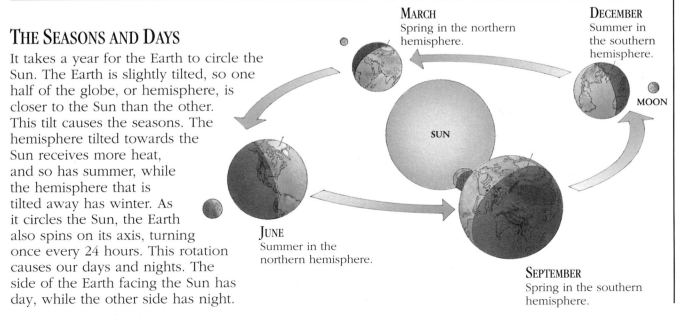

INSIDE THE EARTH

Scientists believe that the Earth was formed about 4,600 million years ago from a spinning cloud of gas and dust, which shrank to form a hot ball of liquid, or molten, rock. As it cooled, the Earth's surface formed into a solid crust. Under the surface the temperature is so high that parts of the Earth are still liquid. Movement of this molten material in the outer core is thought to produce the Earth's magnetic fields.

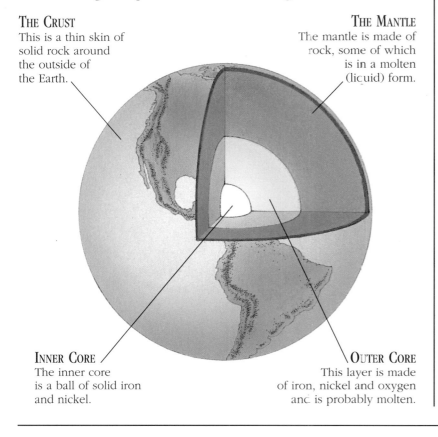

THE CRUST
This is a thin skin of solid rock around the outside of the Earth.

THE MANTLE
The mantle is made of rock, some of which is in a molten (liquid) form.

INNER CORE
The inner core is a ball of solid iron and nickel.

OUTER CORE
This layer is made of iron, nickel and oxygen and is probably molten.

THE WANDERING CONTINENTS

The Earth's crust is made up of pieces called plates, which float on top of a layer of molten rock in the mantle. There are seven main plates and several smaller ones. The magnetic forces within the Earth move the plates slowly around the globe in an ever-changing jigsaw.

Geologists believe that about 270 million years ago all the land on Earth was joined together in one "super-continent", which they call Pangaea. But, as the plates moved around, the land in this super-continent slowly started to split up. This movement is called continental drift. The maps below show how geologists think the continents have moved and split apart to form the landmasses that we know today.

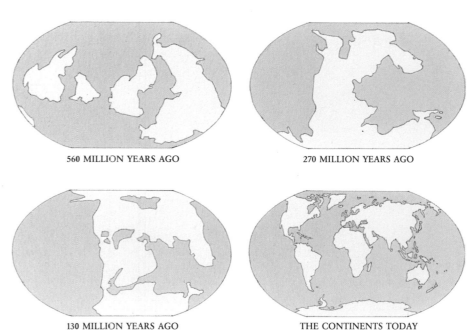

560 MILLION YEARS AGO

270 MILLION YEARS AGO

130 MILLION YEARS AGO

THE CONTINENTS TODAY

THE RESTLESS EARTH

As the plates move around the globe they collide, overlap, and slide past each other. The plates travel very slowly – their fastest speed is about 15 cm (6 in) in a year – but over millions of years the results of this movement can be dramatic. Huge mountain ranges, spectacular rift valleys, and deep trenches in the ocean bed have all been formed in areas where two plates meet. Earthquakes, volcanoes, geysers and hot mud pools are also caused by plate movements. The regions in the world where they are found closely follow the joins between the plates.

SLIDING PAST
The San Andreas Fault in California is an example of a place where two plates are sliding past each other. The sliding movement often occurs in short bursts which are felt on the surface as earthquakes.

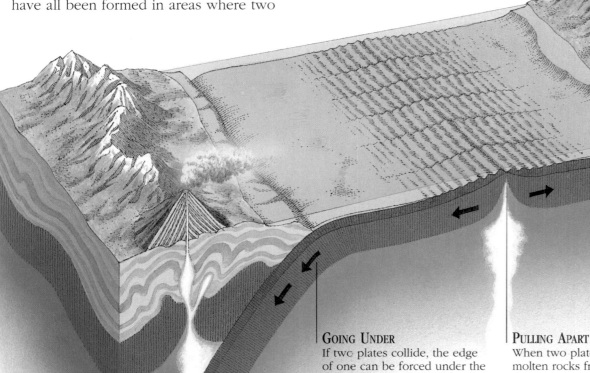

GOING UNDER
If two plates collide, the edge of one can be forced under the other into the mantle below, forming a deep ocean trench. The rocks from the crust melt in the mantle. Often these molten rocks force their way to the surface to form volcanoes.

PULLING APART
When two plates pull apart, molten rocks from the mantle come up to fill the gap. If this happens on the ocean floor it creates underwater mountain ridges. On land, it forms steep-sided valleys, such as the Great Rift Valley in East Africa.

COLLISION COURSE
Sometimes when two plates collide rocks are forced up to form great mountain ranges. These mountains are often volcanic. The Andes range in South America and the Himalayas in Asia were both formed by colliding plates.

Climates Around the World

CLIMATE is the name given to the typical weather conditions and temperature in a particular area. Similar types of climate are found in different places around the world. For example, there are regions of hot, dry desert in Africa, North America, and central Australia.

The climate in any particular place depends partly on its latitude, that is, how far north or south of the Equator it lies. The regions around the Equator are the hottest places in the world. The further away from the Equator you go, the colder the climate becomes. The coldest places in the world are the polar regions around the North and South Poles.

Climate is also affected by how close a place is to the sea. The sea warms and cools the land near it, so coastal areas usually have fewer extremes of temperature than places in the centre of a continent. Another important influence is altitude – how high a place is above sea level. The higher the place, the colder is its climate.

Polar and Tundra Regions
The areas round the North and South Poles are covered in ice. The temperature only rises above freezing point for a few months of the year. South of the North Pole lie regions known as the tundra, where the lower parts of the soil are permanently frozen and only mosses and lichens can grow. As the climate is very dry, the tundra regions are sometimes described as cold deserts.

During the short summer period, the edges of the polar ice caps melt. Large pieces of ice break off and form icebergs.

Mountain Regions
The temperature in mountainous regions varies a lot – the higher up you go, the colder it becomes. Trees and plants often grow on the lower slopes of mountains, but above a certain height (known as the tree line), temperatures are too low for vegetation to survive. Still higher up is the snow line. Above this it is so cold that the ground is permanently covered by snow and ice.

Mount Kilimanjaro in Kenya lies almost on the Equator, but it is so high that its peak is covered in snow all year round.

Taiga
Taiga is a Russian word which means "cold forest". It is used to describe the huge areas of evergreen forest that stretch across northern parts of Canada, Scandinavia, and the USSR. Evergreen trees, such as spruces, pines and firs, are the only type of vegetation that can survive in the long, snowy winters and short summers of this type of climate.

The trees in the taiga regions are an important source of wealth. They are used for timber and for making paper.

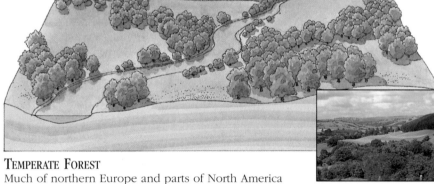

Temperate Forest
Much of northern Europe and parts of North America have a temperate climate, which means that the temperature is never very hot or very cold. Because these regions have rainfall throughout the year, they were once covered by forests. Most of these have now been cut down. Deciduous trees, which shed their leaves in the winter, are common in temperate regions.

Much of the land in northern Europe has been cleared for farming, and small pockets of trees are all that is left of the forests.

The Ocean Floor
The ocean floor is not flat. Like the land, it has many geographical features, such as mountain ranges, flat plains and deep trenches. The longest range of mountains in the world is the underwater Indian Ocean–Pacific Ocean Cordillera. It stretches from East Africa, through the Indian Ocean, round southern Australia, and across the Pacific Ocean to the Gulf of California – a distance of 30,900 km (19,200 miles). The deepest point in the oceans, the Mariana trench in the Pacific Ocean near Japan, is about 11,034 m (36,201 ft) below sea level – deeper than the height of Mount Everest. The shallowest parts of the oceans are the areas of seabed around the edges of the continents, which are called the continental shelves.

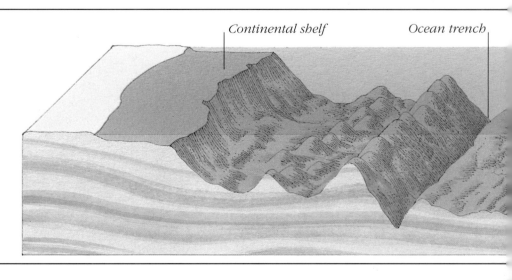

Continental shelf

Ocean trench

MEDITERRANEAN

The name "Mediterranean" is given to the type of climate which is found around the Mediterranean Sea, and in other similar regions of the world, such as California in North America. These areas have hot, dry summers and cool, wet winters. The trees and plants that grow there are specially adapted to survive the lack of water in summer.

Olive trees are one of the few plants that thrive in this climate. They have been cultivated around the Mediterranean for many centuries.

DRY GRASSLAND

In the middle of some of the continents are huge plains of grassland, such as the North American Prairies, the Russian Steppe, and the Argentinian Pampas. These regions have extreme climates – very hot summers and very cold winters. Large parts of these areas have now been taken over for farming and are used for growing wheat or raising cattle.

South American farmers raise large numbers of beef cattle on the grassy plains of the Pampas.

HOT DESERT

The hottest and driest climates in the world are found in the tropical deserts, such as the Sahara in Africa and the Australian Outback. The temperature there often reaches 38° C (100° F) in the shade. In some desert areas there may be no rain for several years. Deserts often contain sandy soil that can only support plants such as cacti, which are adapted to the dry conditions.

The dry, desert plains of the Australian Outback cover more than two-thirds of the continent. Few plants and animals can survive there.

TROPICAL GRASSLAND

Between the wet equatorial rainforests and the hot dry deserts lie regions of tropical grassland, such as the African Savannah. Here the climate is always hot, but the year divides between a dry and a wet season. Tall grasses and low trees and bushes grow in these areas. Tropical grasslands are grazed by large herds of plant-eating animals

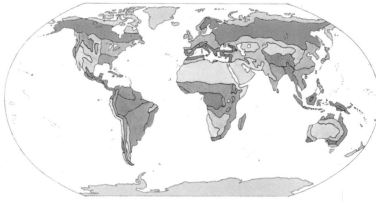

The African Savannah is the last place on Earth where huge herds of grazing animals, such as zebra, gazelles, and wildebeest, still survive.

EQUATORIAL RAINFOREST

In the regions around the Equator, the climate is hot and wet all year round. The temperature remains constant at about 27–28° C (80–82° F). Vegetation thrives in this type of climate, and the equatorial regions used to be covered in dense rainforest. Much of this has now been cut down, although large areas still remain in the Amazon river basin in South America.

The Amazon rainforest covers an area 12 times the size of France. It is home to more species of birds and animals than anywhere else on Earth.

WHERE CLIMATES ARE FOUND

▢ Polar and tundra	▢ Temperate forest	▢ Hot desert
▢ Mountain regions	▢ Mediterranean	▢ Tropical grassland
▢ Taiga	▢ Dry grassland	▢ Rainforest

Mid-ocean ridge

Volcanic island

The Countries of the World

ALL OF THE CONTINENTS except Antarctica are divided into different countries, and these vary in size. By far the largest country in the world is the USSR, which stretches across two continents – Europe and Asia. The second largest country is Canada and the third largest is China. At the other end of the scale, the smallest country is the Vatican City, which lies in the city of Rome in Italy. It has a total area of only 0.44 sq km (0.17 sq mile). The USSR is more than 50 million times bigger than the Vatican City.

Latitude and Longitude

To help locate places in the world, geographers draw imaginary lines around the globe. Lines of latitude circle the globe from east to west. They are measured in degrees north or south of the Equator. Lines of longitude circle the Earth from north to south and are measured in degrees east or west of the line called the Prime Meridian.

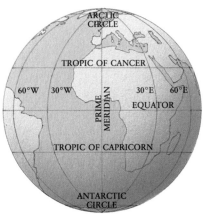

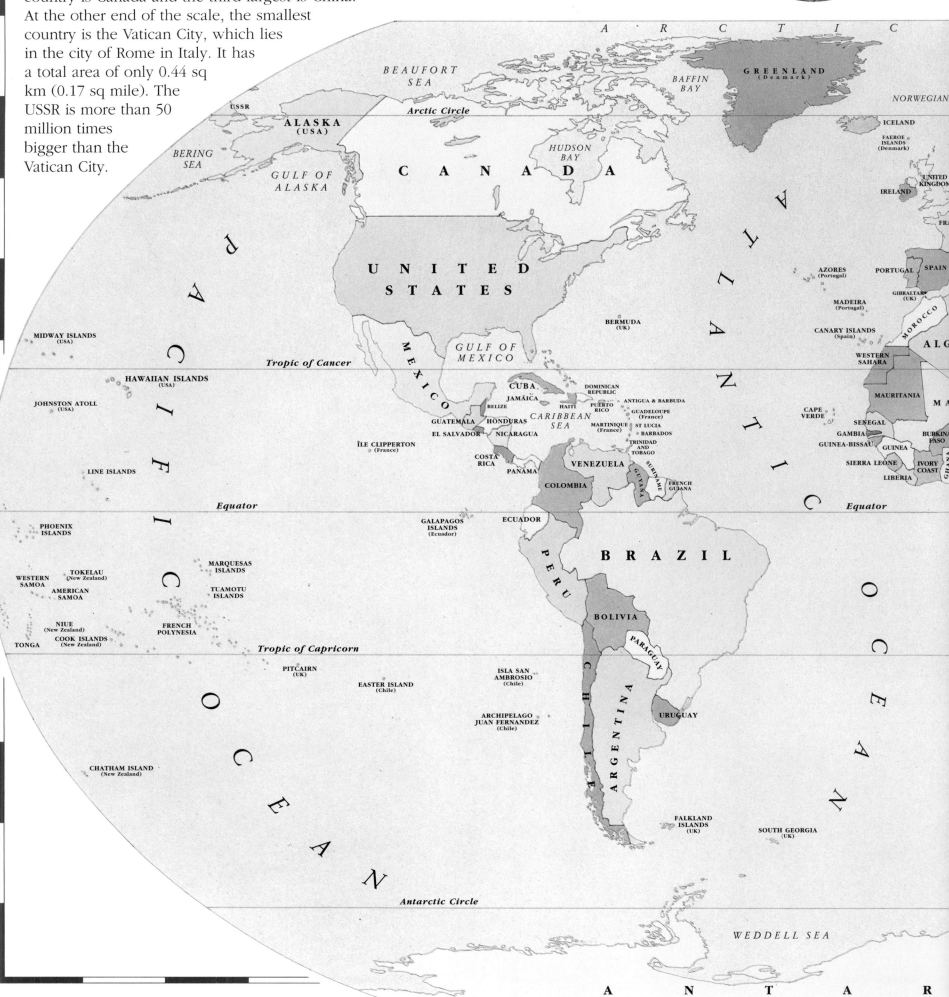

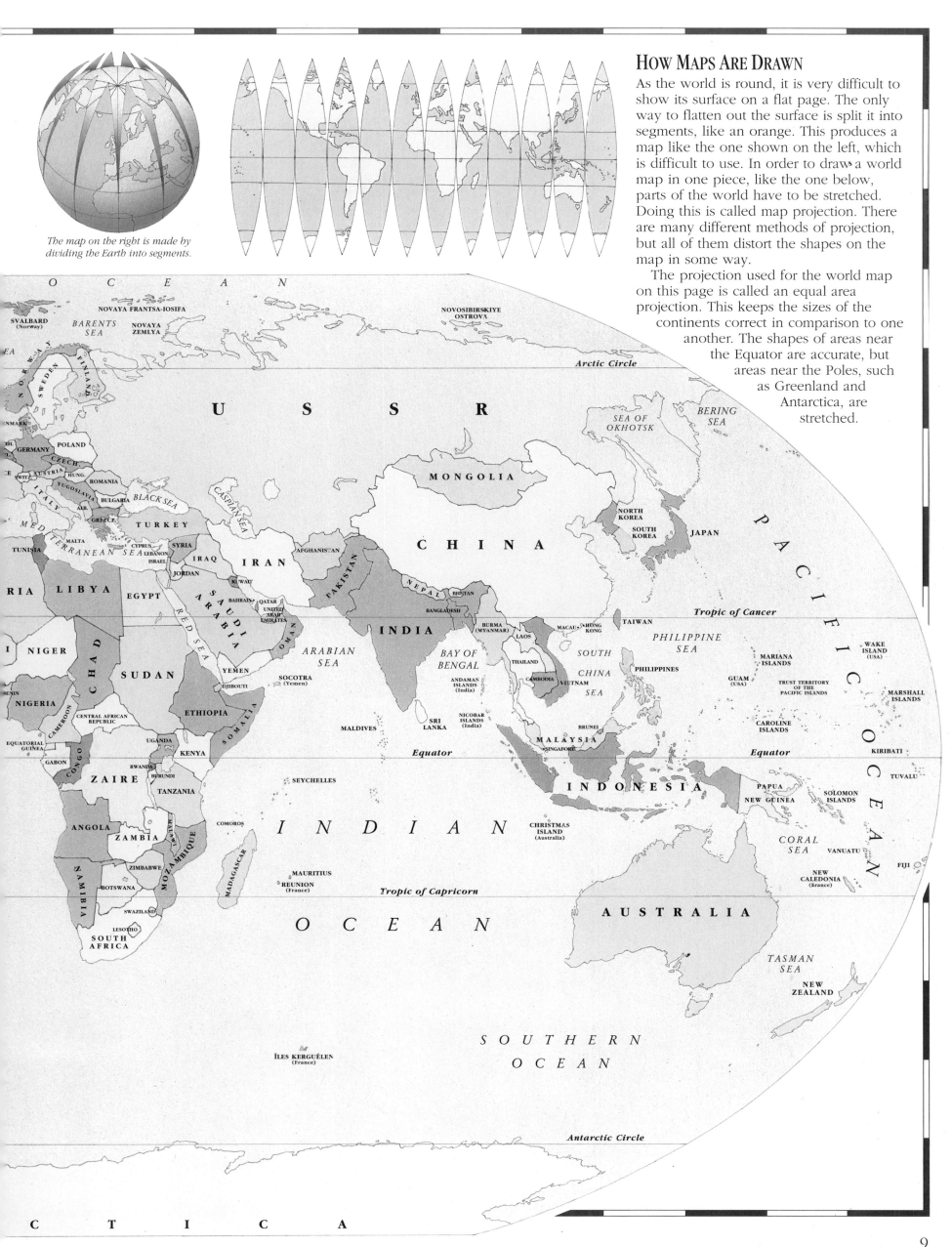

HOW MAPS ARE DRAWN

As the world is round, it is very difficult to show its surface on a flat page. The only way to flatten out the surface is split it into segments, like an orange. This produces a map like the one shown on the left, which is difficult to use. In order to draw a world map in one piece, like the one below, parts of the world have to be stretched. Doing this is called map projection. There are many different methods of projection, but all of them distort the shapes on the map in some way.

The projection used for the world map on this page is called an equal area projection. This keeps the sizes of the continents correct in comparison to one another. The shapes of areas near the Equator are accurate, but areas near the Poles, such as Greenland and Antarctica, are stretched.

The map on the right is made by dividing the Earth into segments.

Arctic Circle

O C E A N

SVALBARD (Norway)
NOVAYA FRANTSA-IOSIFA
NOVAYA ZEMLYA
BARENTS SEA
NOVOSIBIRSKIYE OSTROVA

U S S R

NORWAY
SWEDEN
FINLAND
DENMARK
GERMANY
POLAND
CZECH.
SWITZ. AUSTRIA HUNG.
ITALY
YUGOSLAVIA
ROMANIA
BULGARIA
BLACK SEA
ALB.
GREECE
TURKEY
CASPIAN SEA
MONGOLIA
SEA OF OKHOTSK
BERING SEA

MED TERRANEAN SEA
MALTA
TUNISIA
CYPRUS
LEBANON
SYRIA
IRAQ
ISRAEL
JORDAN
KUWAIT
IRAN
AFGHANISTAN
PAKISTAN
CHINA
NORTH KOREA
SOUTH KOREA
JAPAN

P A C I F I C   O C E A N

RIA
LIBYA
EGYPT
SAUDI ARABIA
BAHRAIN
QATAR
UNITED ARAB EMIRATES
OMAN
RED SEA
NEPAL
BHUTAN
BANGLADESH
Tropic of Cancer

I
NIGER
CHAD
SUDAN
YEMEN
ARABIAN SEA
INDIA
BAY OF BENGAL
BURMA (MYANMAR)
LAOS
THAILAND
MACAU
HONG KONG
TAIWAN
PHILIPPINE SEA
MARIANA ISLANDS
WAKE ISLAND (USA)

BENIN
NIGERIA
CAMEROON
CENTRAL AFRICAN REPUBLIC
ETHIOPIA
SOMALIA
DJIBOUTI
SOCOTRA (Yemen)
ANDAMAN ISLANDS (India)
CAMBODIA
VIETNAM
SOUTH CHINA SEA
PHILIPPINES
GUAM (USA)
TRUST TERRITORY OF THE PACIFIC ISLANDS
MARSHALL ISLANDS

EQUATORIAL GUINEA
GABON
CONGO
ZAIRE
UGANDA
RWANDA
BURUNDI
KENYA
TANZANIA
MALDIVES
SRI LANKA
NICOBAR ISLANDS (India)
BRUNEI
MALAYSIA
SINGAPORE
CAROLINE ISLANDS
Equator
Equator
KIRIBATI

ANGOLA
ZAMBIA
ZIMBABWE
MOZAMBIQUE
COMOROS
SEYCHELLES
I N D I A N
INDONESIA
PAPUA NEW GUINEA
SOLOMON ISLANDS
TUVALU

NAMIBIA
BOTSWANA
MALAWI
MADAGASCAR
MAURITIUS
REUNION (France)
CHRISTMAS ISLAND (Australia)
CORAL SEA
VANUATU
NEW CALEDONIA (France)
FIJI

SWAZILAND
LESOTHO
SOUTH AFRICA
Tropic of Capricorn

O C E A N
A U S T R A L I A
TASMAN SEA
NEW ZEALAND

ÎLES KERGUÉLEN (France)
S O U T H E R N   O C E A N

Antarctic Circle

C T I C A

9

THE BIGGEST, HIGHEST, AND LONGEST ON EARTH

WHAT IS THE LONGEST river on Earth? How high is Mount Everest? Which is the world's biggest island? You can find the answers to all these questions below. Each of the sections is about one type of geographical feature

– mountains, for example. The section contains the highest mountain on Earth – Mt Everest – along with a selection of other mountains from around the world.

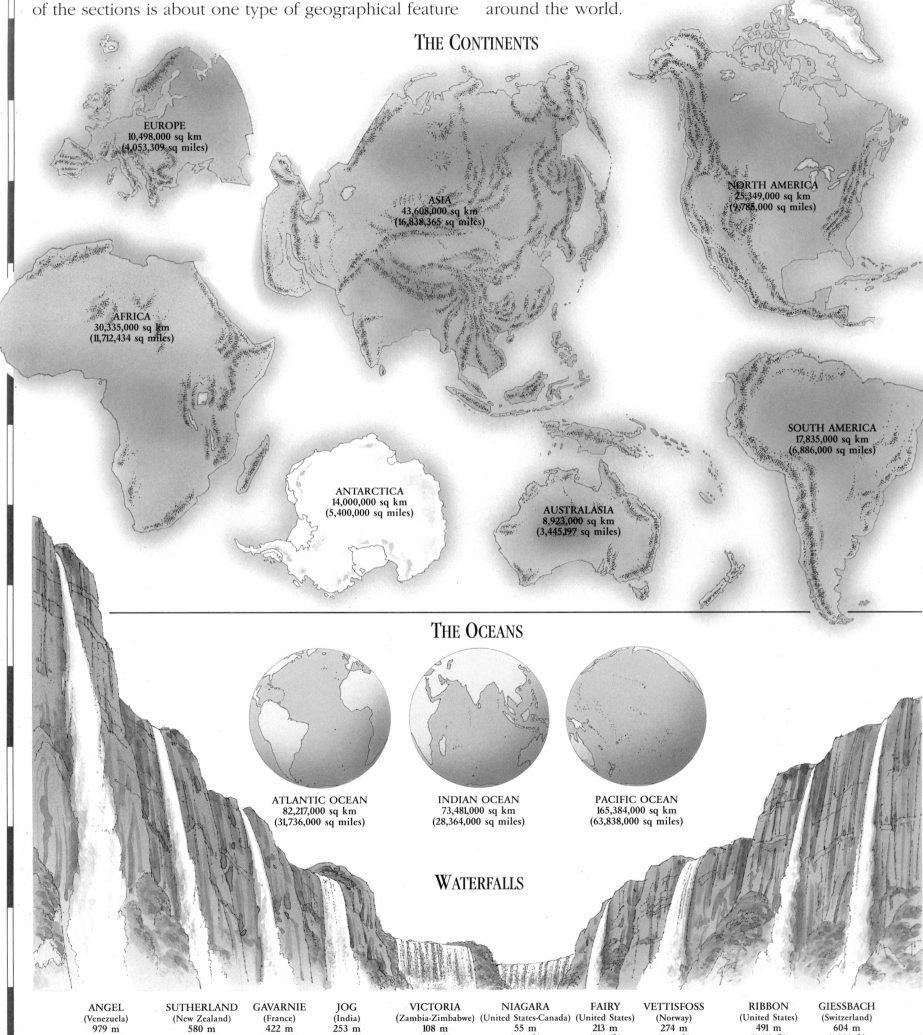

THE CONTINENTS

EUROPE
10,498,000 sq km
(4,053,309 sq miles)

ASIA
43,608,000 sq km
(16,838,365 sq miles)

NORTH AMERICA
25,349,000 sq km
(9,785,000 sq miles)

AFRICA
30,335,000 sq km
(11,712,434 sq miles)

SOUTH AMERICA
17,835,000 sq km
(6,886,000 sq miles)

ANTARCTICA
14,000,000 sq km
(5,400,000 sq miles)

AUSTRALASIA
8,923,000 sq km
(3,445,197 sq miles)

THE OCEANS

ATLANTIC OCEAN
82,217,000 sq km
(31,736,000 sq miles)

INDIAN OCEAN
73,481,000 sq km
(28,364,000 sq miles)

PACIFIC OCEAN
165,384,000 sq km
(63,838,000 sq miles)

WATERFALLS

ANGEL (Venezuela)	SUTHERLAND (New Zealand)	GAVARNIE (France)	JOG (India)	VICTORIA (Zambia-Zimbabwe)	NIAGARA (United States-Canada)	FAIRY (United States)	VETTISFOSS (Norway)	RIBBON (United States)	GIESSBACH (Switzerland)
979 m (3,212 ft)	580 m (1,904 ft)	422 m (1,385 ft)	253 m (830 ft)	108 m (355 ft)	55 m (182 ft)	213 m (700 ft)	274 m (900 ft)	491 m (1,612 ft)	604 m (1,982 ft)

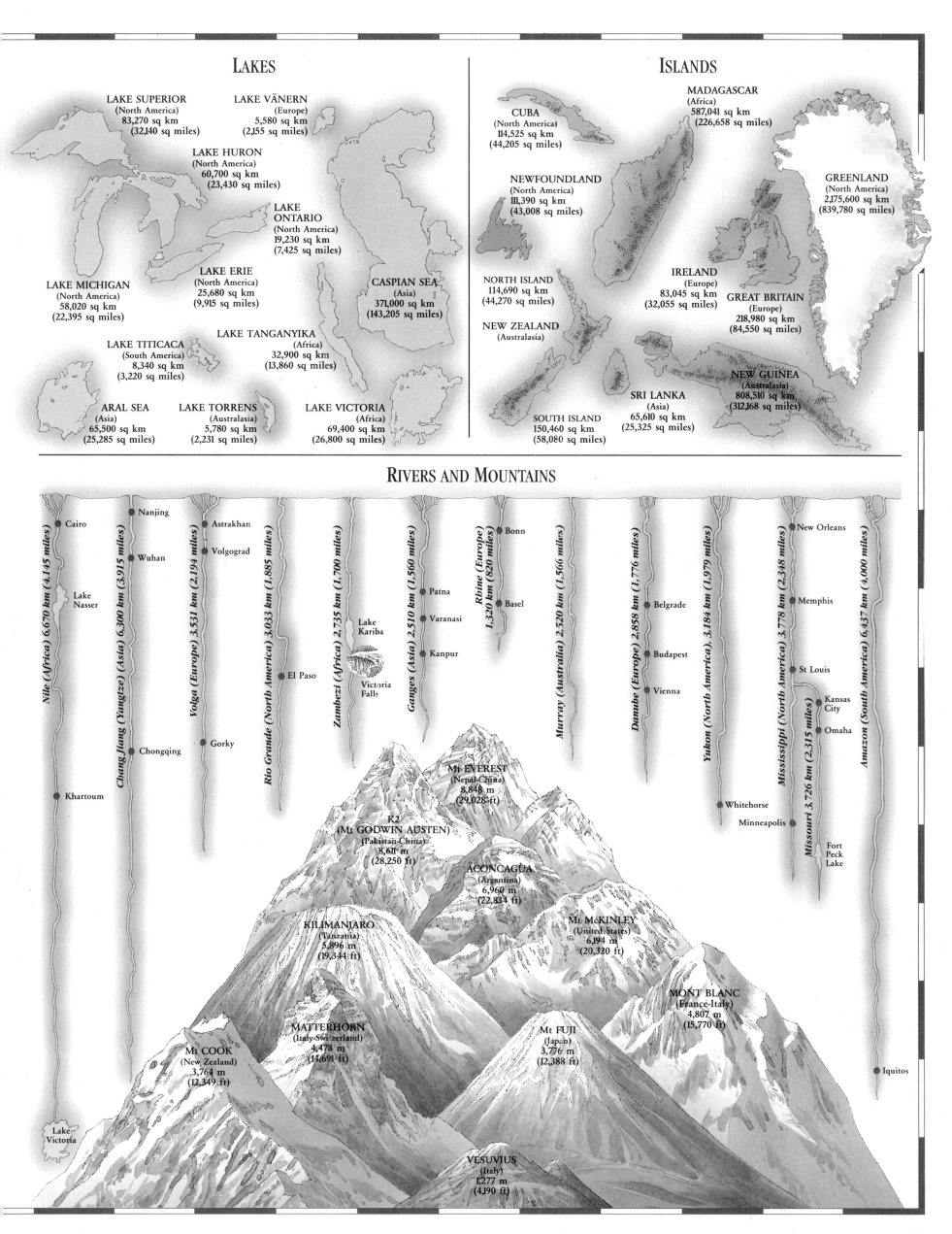

LAKES

LAKE SUPERIOR
(North America)
83,270 sq km
(32,140 sq miles)

LAKE VÄNERN
(Europe)
5,580 sq km
(2,155 sq miles)

LAKE HURON
(North America)
60,700 sq km
(23,430 sq miles)

LAKE ONTARIO
(North America)
19,230 sq km
(7,425 sq miles)

LAKE MICHIGAN
(North America)
58,020 sq km
(22,395 sq miles)

LAKE ERIE
(North America)
25,680 sq km
(9,915 sq miles)

CASPIAN SEA
(Asia)
371,000 sq km
(143,205 sq miles)

LAKE TANGANYIKA
(Africa)
32,900 sq km
(13,860 sq miles)

LAKE TITICACA
(South America)
8,340 sq km
(3,220 sq miles)

ARAL SEA
(Asia)
65,500 sq km
(25,285 sq miles)

LAKE TORRENS
(Australasia)
5,780 sq km
(2,231 sq miles)

LAKE VICTORIA
(Africa)
69,400 sq km
(26,800 sq miles)

ISLANDS

MADAGASCAR
(Africa)
587,041 sq km
(226,658 sq miles)

CUBA
(North America)
114,525 sq km
(44,205 sq miles)

NEWFOUNDLAND
(North America)
111,390 sq km
(43,008 sq miles)

GREENLAND
(North America)
2,175,600 sq km
(839,780 sq miles)

NORTH ISLAND
114,690 sq km
(44,270 sq miles)

NEW ZEALAND
(Australasia)

IRELAND
(Europe)
83,045 sq km
(32,055 sq miles)

GREAT BRITAIN
(Europe)
218,980 sq km
(84,550 sq miles)

NEW GUINEA
(Australasia)
808,510 sq km
(312,168 sq miles)

SOUTH ISLAND
150,460 sq km
(58,080 sq miles)

SRI LANKA
(Asia)
65,610 sq km
(25,325 sq miles)

RIVERS AND MOUNTAINS

Nile (Africa) 6,670 km (4,145 miles) — Cairo, Lake Nasser, Khartoum

Chang Jiang (Yangtze) (Asia) 6,300 km (3,915 miles) — Nanjing, Wuhan, Chongqing

Volga (Europe) 3,531 km (2,194 miles) — Astrakhan, Volgograd, Gorky

Rio Grande (North America) 3,033 km (1,885 miles) — El Paso

Zambezi (Africa) 2,735 km (1,700 miles) — Lake Kariba, Victoria Falls

Ganges (Asia) 2,510 km (1,560 miles) — Patna, Varanasi, Kanpur

Rhine (Europe) 1,320 km (820 miles) — Bonn, Basel

Murray (Australia) 2,520 km (1,566 miles)

Danube (Europe) 2,858 km (1,776 miles) — Belgrade, Budapest, Vienna

Yukon (North America) 3,184 km (1,979 miles) — Whitehorse

Mississippi (North America) 3,778 km (2,348 miles) — New Orleans, Memphis, St Louis, Minneapolis

Missouri 3,726 km (2,315 miles) — Kansas City, Omaha, Fort Peck Lake

Amazon (South America) 6,437 km (4,000 miles) — Iquitos

Mt EVEREST
(Nepal-China)
8,848 m
(29,028 ft)

K2
(Mt GODWIN AUSTEN)
(Pakistan-China)
8,611 m
(28,250 ft)

ACONCAGUA
(Argentina)
6,960 m
(22,834 ft)

Mt McKINLEY
(United States)
6,194 m
(20,320 ft)

KILIMANJARO
(Tanzania)
5,896 m
(19,344 ft)

MONT BLANC
(France-Italy)
4,807 m
(15,770 ft)

MATTERHORN
(Italy-Switzerland)
4,478 m
(14,691 ft)

Mt FUJI
(Japan)
3,776 m
(12,388 ft)

Mt COOK
(New Zealand)
3,764 m
(12,349 ft)

Lake Victoria

VESUVIUS
(Italy)
1,277 m
(4,190 ft)

WHERE PEOPLE LIVE

THE TOTAL POPULATION of the world is more than 5,000 million people. No-one knows the exact figure, as it is constantly rising. The population of the world is growing faster now than ever before. It has doubled since 1950, and many experts believe that it will double again within the next 40 years.

The population of the world is not spread evenly around the globe. Many of the most densely populated countries are in Europe and Asia. In the Netherlands, for example, an average of 360 people live in each square kilometre of land. In contrast, Australia has an average of only two people per square kilometre.

POPULATION BY CONTINENT

The diagrams below show how many people live in each of the continents. Antarctica is the only continent which has no permanent population: the only people who live there are scientists and engineers.

👤 = 10 million people

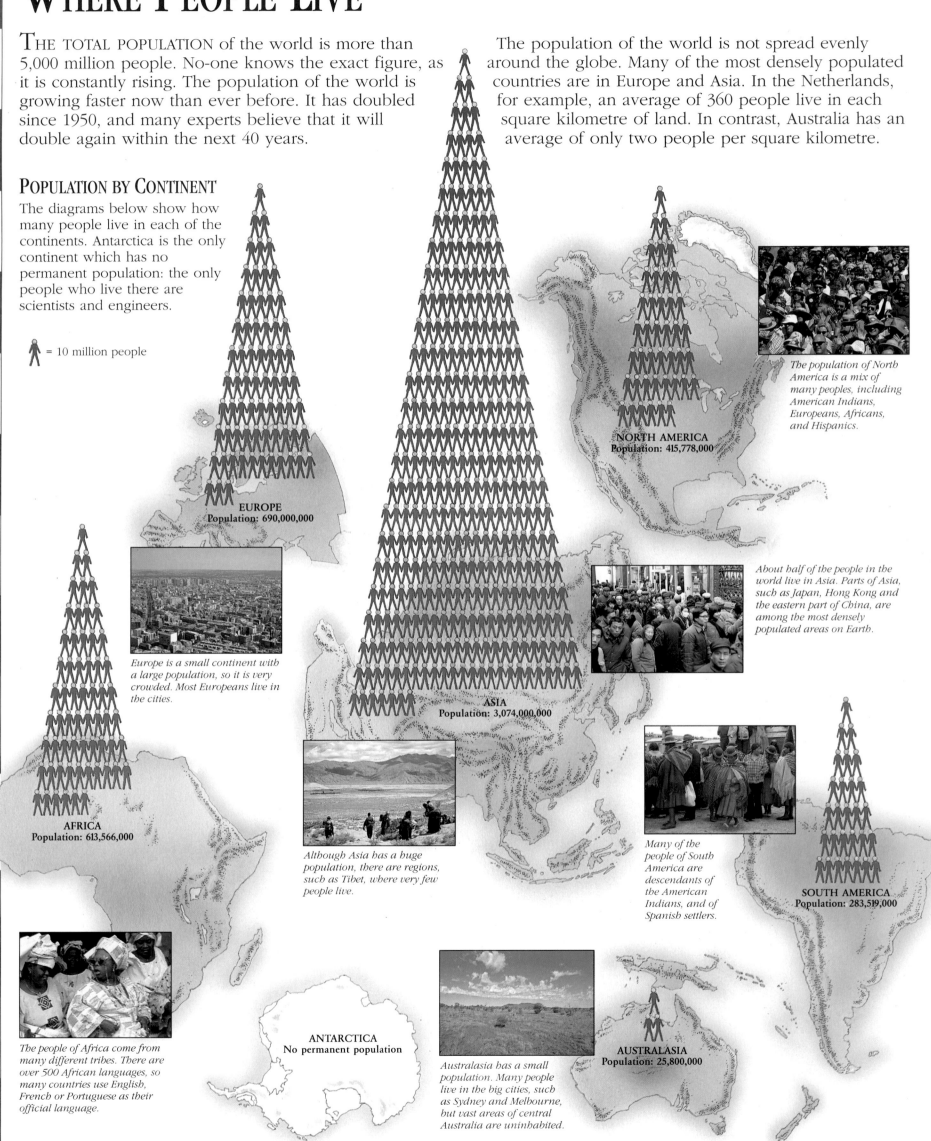

EUROPE
Population: 690,000,000

Europe is a small continent with a large population, so it is very crowded. Most Europeans live in the cities.

AFRICA
Population: 613,566,000

The people of Africa come from many different tribes. There are over 500 African languages, so many countries use English, French or Portuguese as their official language.

ASIA
Population: 3,074,000,000

Although Asia has a huge population, there are regions, such as Tibet, where very few people live.

ANTARCTICA
No permanent population

NORTH AMERICA
Population: 415,778,000

The population of North America is a mix of many peoples, including American Indians, Europeans, Africans, and Hispanics.

About half of the people in the world live in Asia. Parts of Asia, such as Japan, Hong Kong and the eastern part of China, are among the most densely populated areas on Earth.

Many of the people of South America are descendants of the American Indians, and of Spanish settlers.

SOUTH AMERICA
Population: 283,519,000

Australasia has a small population. Many people live in the big cities, such as Sydney and Melbourne, but vast areas of central Australia are uninhabited.

AUSTRALASIA
Population: 25,800,000

HOW TO USE THIS ATLAS

THE MAPS IN THIS ATLAS are split into a number of sections. There is one section for each of the continents: Antarctica, North America, South America, Europe, Asia, Africa, and Australasia. At the start of each section is a map of the whole continent, like the one of North America shown at the bottom of this page. Following this are a series of regional maps, like the one of France below, which show all the countries in that continent. This page shows how to use these maps and explains what the symbols on the maps mean.

NATIONAL FLAGS
The flags of all the countries on the map are shown like this.

BORDERING COUNTRIES
Countries which lie around the edges of the area shown on the map are coloured yellow.

USING THE GRID
The grid around the outside of the page helps you to find places on the map. For example, to find the city of Paris, look its name up in the index on pages 77–80. Next to the word Paris are the reference numbers 39 E13. The first number shows that Paris is on page 39 of the atlas. The second number means that it is in square E13 of the grid. Turn to page 39. Trace across from the letter E on the grid and then down from the number 13. Paris is situated in the area where the two meet.

WHERE ON EARTH?
The red area on the globe shows where the countries on the map are situated.

FACTS AND FIGURES
This box contains interesting facts and statistics about each of the countries on the map.

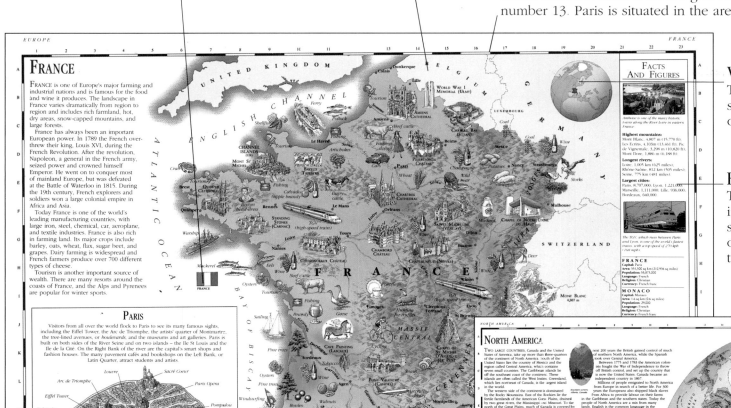

SPECIAL FEATURES
Features like this one give further information about a place or feature of interest on the map.

SCALE
You can use the scale to see how big the countries are, and how far it is from one place to another. Not all the maps have been drawn to the same scale.

POLITICAL MAP
This shows all the countries in the continent.

GEOGRAPHICAL MAP
This map of the continent shows all the main geographical features, such as rivers, mountains, lakes and deserts.

KEY TO THE MAPS

Capital City	City	Country name	Range of mountains	An individual mountain with its height	River	Lake	A specific building or place	A product, animal, plant or activity, that is found all over the region
LONDON	Bristol	FRANCE	ALPS	△ MT EVEREST 8,848 m	Ganges	LAKE TITICACA	THE LEANING TOWER OF PISA	Wine

13

THE ARCTIC

THE ARCTIC CIRCLE contains the northernmost parts of North America, Europe and Asia, along with most of the island of Greenland. The temperature in the Arctic is so low that much of the Arctic Ocean is permanently frozen. Within the Arctic Circle, there are days in midwinter when the Sun never rises, and days in midsummer when it never sets. Despite the harsh climate, a wide variety of animals and plants live in the Arctic. The main human inhabitants are the Inuit (Eskimos) and the Sami (Lapps).

The island of Greenland is anything but green – much of it is permanently covered by ice. The Inuit have lived in Greenland since about 2500 BC. The first Europeans to settle there were the Vikings, in about AD 986. Today Greenland is a self-governing province of Denmark.

FACTS AND FIGURES

Flowing river of ice, called a glacier, in Greenland.

Highest mountain:
Mt Gunnbjorn (Greenland), 3,700 m (12,139 ft.)

Beneath the North Pole:
There is no solid land. This was proved in 1958 when a submarine, the USS Nautilus, travelled under the ice.

Flight Paths over the Arctic:
These provide the shortest air connections between Europe and North America.

GREENLAND
Area: 2,175,600 sq km (839,780 sq miles)
Population: 55,000

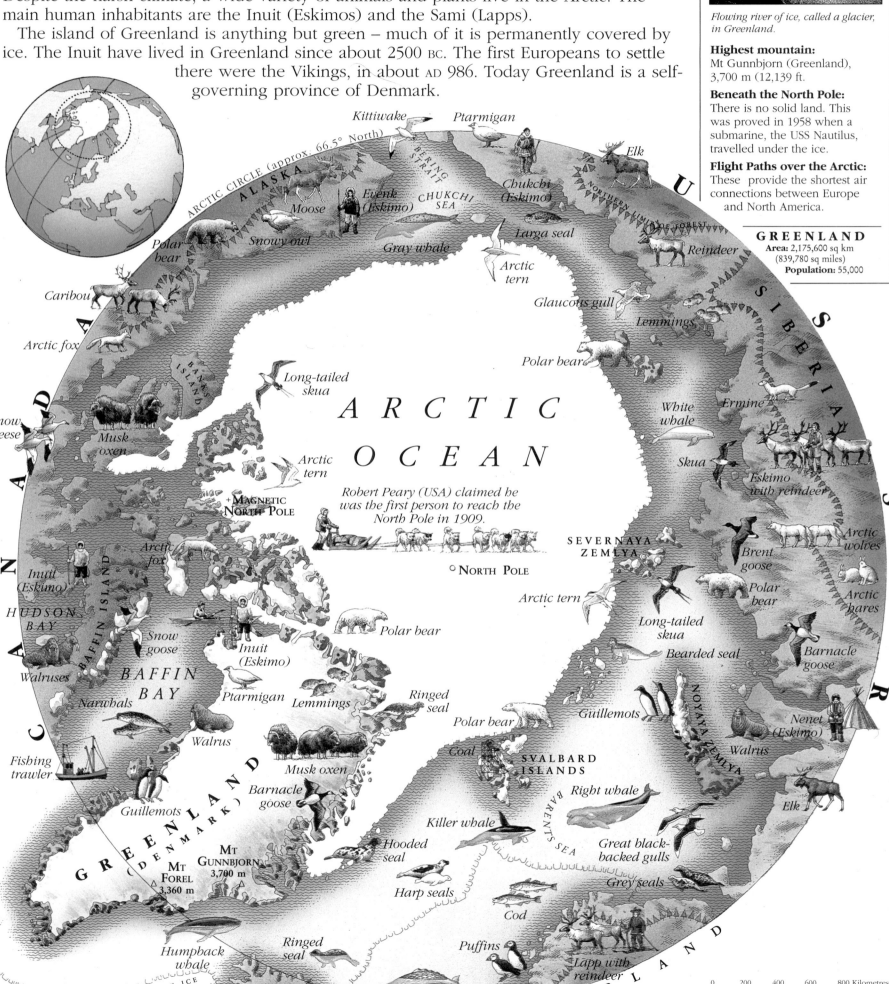

Robert Peary (USA) claimed he was the first person to reach the North Pole in 1909.

THE ANTARCTIC

THE ANTARCTIC has the coldest and harshest climate in the world. Nearly all the land is covered by ice, on average about 2,000 m (6,562 ft) thick. The size of the ice sheet varies between the seasons. In summer the ice at the edge of the sheet melts or breaks off to form icebergs. In winter the sea at the edge of the ice sheet freezes again and is called pack ice. There are very few plants. The animals that live in the Antarctic, such as seals and penguins, depend on the sea for their supply of food.

Although no country owns Antarctica, a number of countries claim territory, and many have bases there for scientific research. Even the small population of scientists dwindles during the bitter Antarctic winter, when blizzards last for days. The world's coldest temperature of -89.2°C (-128.6°F) was recorded at Vostok Station in July 1983.

FACTS AND FIGURES

The sea around the Antarctic is covered by drifting pack ice for most of the year.

Antarctica contains 90 per cent of all the world's ice: If it melted, the level of the seas throughout the world would rise by 60 m (200 ft) and drown all the coastal towns and cities.

CONTINENT OF ANTARCTICA
Area: 14,000,000 sq km (5,400,000 sq miles)
Inhabitants: Scientists and engineers only
Climate: Cold, dry and windy

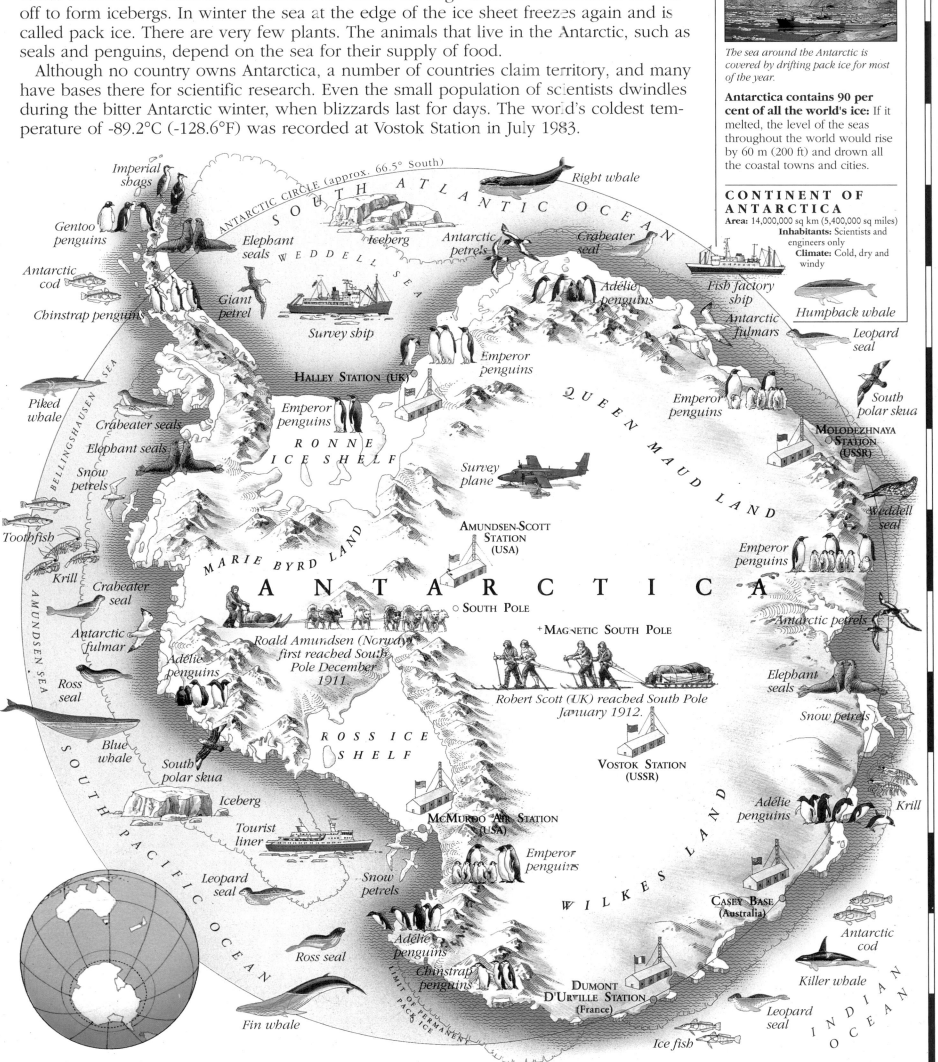

15

NORTH AMERICA

TWO LARGE COUNTRIES, Canada and the United States of America, take up more than three-quarters of the continent of North America. South of the United States lies the country of Mexico and the region called Central America, which contains seven small countries. The Caribbean islands lie off the southeast coast of the continent. These islands are often called the West Indies. Greenland, which lies northeast of Canada, is the largest island in the world.

Mountain scenery, Alberta, Canada.

The western side of the continent is dominated by the Rocky Mountains. East of the Rockies lie the fertile farmlands of the American Great Plains, drained by two great rivers, the Mississippi and Missouri. To the north of the Great Plains, much of Canada is covered by vast regions of pine forest. The northernmost part of the continent lies within the Arctic Circle.

The first settlers crossed to North America from Asia in about 40,000 BC, when Alaska was joined to Siberia by a land bridge. These people were the ancestors of the American Indians.

Ancient Maya city of Palenque, Mexico.

The first Europeans to discover the continent were probably the Vikings in about AD 1000, but Europeans only began to settle there in the 16th century. Over the next 200 years the British gained control of much of northern North America, while the Spanish took over Central America.

Between 1775 and 1783 the American colonists fought the War of Independence to throw off British control, and set up the country that is now the United States. Canada became an independent country in 1867.

Millions of people emigrated to North America from Europe in search of a better life. For 300 years the Europeans also shipped black slaves from Africa to provide labour on their farms in the Caribbean and the southern states. Today the people of North America are a mix from many lands. English is the common language in the United States and most of Canada (although some Canadians speak French), while Spanish is spoken in Mexico and most of Central America.

The Capitol Building, Washington DC, United States.

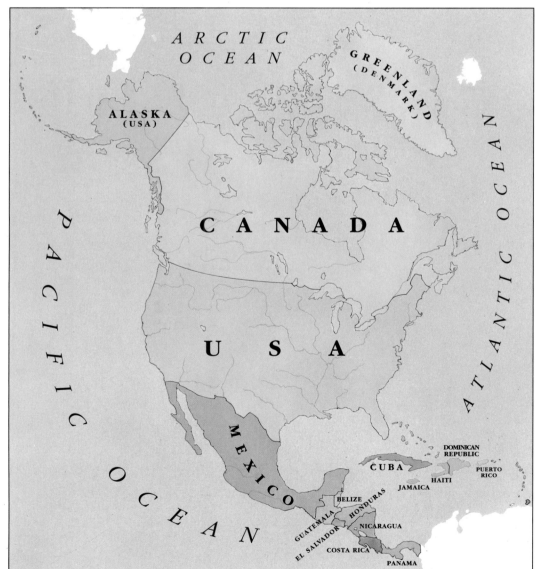

FACTS ABOUT NORTH AMERICA

Area: 25,349,000 sq km (9,785,000 sq miles).

Population: 415,778,000.

Number of independent countries: 23.

Largest countries: Canada, 9,976,139 sq km (3,851,817 sq miles); United States, 9,372,614 sq km (3,618,794 sq miles); Mexico, 1,967,183 sq km (761,530 sq miles).

Most populated countries: United States, 245,871,000; Mexico, 83,593,000.

Largest cities: Mexico City (Mexico), 19,000,000 (the largest city in the world); New York City (United States), 18,054,000; Los Angeles (United States), 13,471,000.

Longest rivers: Mississippi-Missouri, 6,019 km (3,740 miles); Mackenzie, 4,240 km (2,635 miles); Yukon, 3,184 km (1,979 miles).

Highest mountains: Mt McKinley (United States), 6,194 m (20,320 ft); Mt Logan (Canada), 5,951 m (19,524 ft).

Largest lakes: Lake Superior (United States), 83,270 sq km (32,140 sq miles); Lake Huron (United States), 60,700 sq km (23,430 sq miles); Great Bear Lake (Canada), 31,790 sq km (12,270 sq miles).

Largest islands: Greenland, 2,175,600 sq km (839,780 sq miles); Baffin Island, 476,070 sq km (183,760 sq miles).

Hottest place: Death Valley in California (United States) is the hottest place in North America. In 1917 the temperature there reached 48.9°C (120°F).

World's shortest river: The Roe River, which flows into the Missouri near Great Falls in Montana (United States), is only 61m (200 ft) long.

World's highest geyser: Steamboat Geyser in Yellowstone National Park (United States) can reach 115 m (380 ft).

World's longest frontier: The border between Canada and the United States measures 6,416 km (3,987 miles).

CANADA AND ALASKA

CANADA is the world's second largest country, yet its population is small – only about one-tenth the size of the smaller United States, its southern neighbour. More than half of all Canadians live in the area around the Great Lakes and the St Lawrence river. In the centre of Canada lie the Prairies, a flat plain used mainly for grazing cattle and growing wheat. Northern Canada is covered by vast areas of forest and tundra, while the west of the country is dominated by the Rocky Mountains.

The first inhabitants of Canada were the Indian and Inuit (Eskimo) peoples. French and British settlers started to move

there in the 17th century. Although Canada became part of the British Empire, the French influence has always been strong and many Canadians still speak French today. Canada became an independent country in 1867.

Alaska, which lies to the northwest of Canada, is the largest state in the United States. Alaska is one of the world's major oil-producing regions.

MONTREAL

Montreal, situated in the province of Quebec, is one of Canada's largest cities. Two-thirds of the people in Montreal speak French, making it the second largest French-speaking city in the world after Paris. French traders founded the city, which they called Ville-Marie, in 1642. It was built on Montreal Island in the St Lawrence river. Today, Montreal is Canada's leading port and a major trading and manufacturing centre.

Map labels

ARCTIC OCEAN

BERING STRAIT

BEAUFORT SEA

Ice-breaker ship

Polar bear

QUEEN ELIZABETH ISLANDS

Oil

Oil

Caribou

Snow geese

BANKS ISLAND

BERING SEA

Dog-drawn sledge

VICTORIA ISLAND

Musk ox

UNITED STATES

Salmon

ALASKA (USA)

Yukon

Fairbanks

Oil

Arctic fox

Spruce

Furs

Fur seal

Walruses

MT MCKINLEY 6,194 m

Dall sheep

Anchorage

Zinc and lead

GREAT BEAR LAKE

Wolves

Right whale

Oil tanker

MT LOGAN 5,951 m

YUKON TERRITORY

Whitehorse

MACKENZIE MTS

Mackenzie

Silver

NORTHWEST TERR

Yellowknife

Paper birch

Moose

PACIFIC

Juneau

GREAT SLAVE LAKE

ROCKY MTS

Douglas fir

Skiing

peace

LAKE ATHABASCA

COAST MTS

BRITISH COLUMBIA

ALBERTA

Mountie

Grizzly bear

Oil

Salmon

QUEEN CHARLOTTE ISLANDS

Indian totem pole

Edmonton

Calgary skyline

SASKATCHEWAN

Halibut

Calgary

VANCOUVER ISLAND

Fraser

Wheat

Regina

Vancouver

Victoria

The Calgary Stampede (annual rodeo)

OCEAN

0   200   400   600   800 Kilometres

0   100   200   300   400   500 Miles

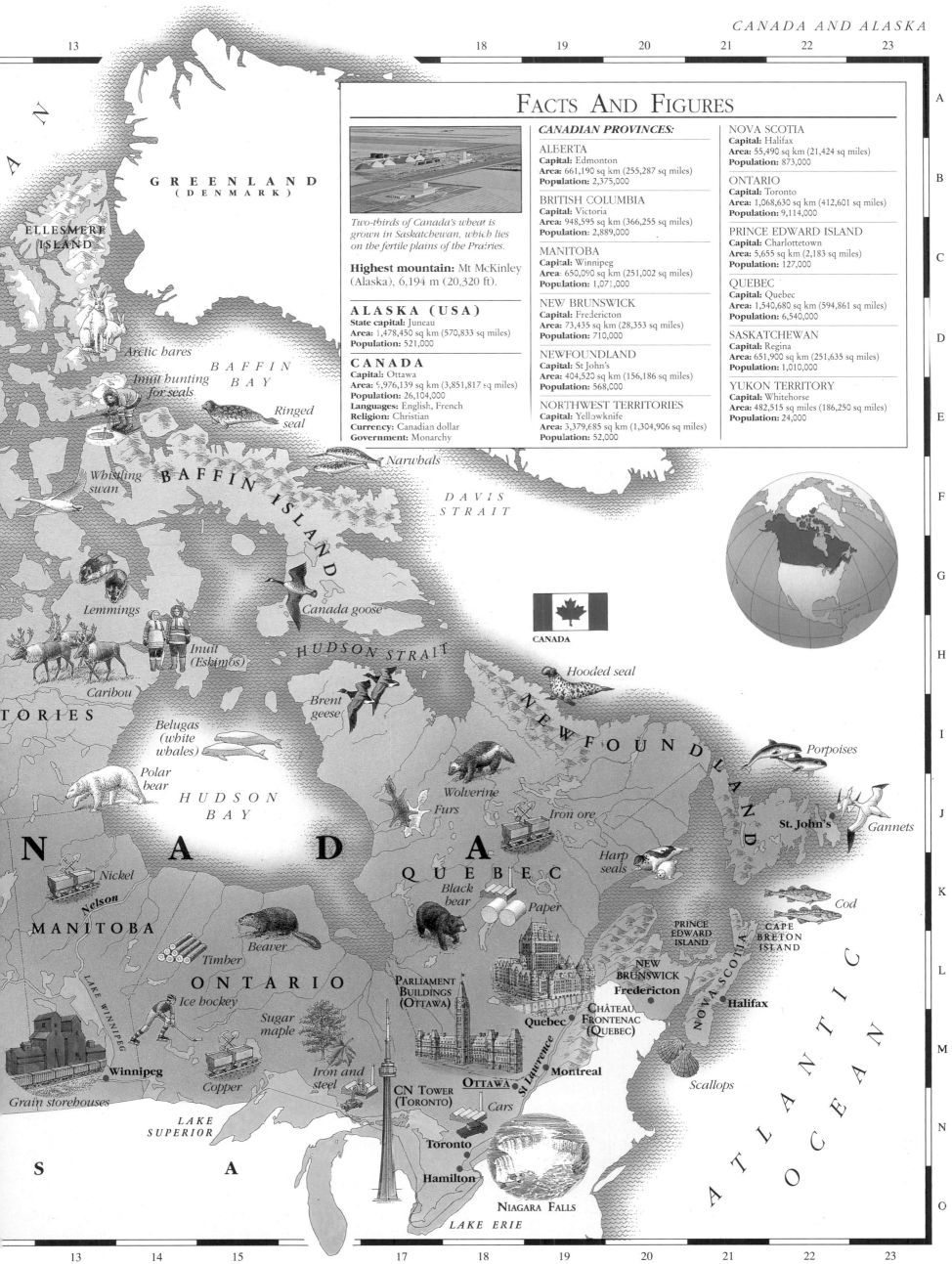

GREENLAND
(DENMARK)

ELLESMERE
ISLAND

FACTS AND FIGURES

Two-thirds of Canada's wheat is grown in Saskatchewan, which lies on the fertile plains of the Prairies.

Highest mountain: Mt McKinley (Alaska), 6,194 m (20,320 ft).

ALASKA (USA)
State capital: Juneau
Area: 1,478,450 sq km (570,833 sq miles)
Population: 521,000

CANADA
Capital: Ottawa
Area: 9,976,139 sq km (3,851,817 sq miles)
Population: 26,104,000
Languages: English, French
Religion: Christian
Currency: Canadian dollar
Government: Monarchy

CANADIAN PROVINCES:

ALBERTA
Capital: Edmonton
Area: 661,190 sq km (255,287 sq miles)
Population: 2,375,000

BRITISH COLUMBIA
Capital: Victoria
Area: 948,595 sq km (366,255 sq miles)
Population: 2,889,000

MANITOBA
Capital: Winnipeg
Area: 650,090 sq km (251,002 sq miles)
Population: 1,071,000

NEW BRUNSWICK
Capital: Fredericton
Area: 73,435 sq km (28,353 sq miles)
Population: 710,000

NEWFOUNDLAND
Capital: St John's
Area: 404,520 sq km (156,186 sq miles)
Population: 568,000

NORTHWEST TERRITORIES
Capital: Yellowknife
Area: 3,379,685 sq km (1,304,906 sq miles)
Population: 52,000

NOVA SCOTIA
Capital: Halifax
Area: 55,490 sq km (21,424 sq miles)
Population: 873,000

ONTARIO
Capital: Toronto
Area: 1,068,630 sq km (412,601 sq miles)
Population: 9,114,000

PRINCE EDWARD ISLAND
Capital: Charlottetown
Area: 5,655 sq km (2,183 sq miles)
Population: 127,000

QUEBEC
Capital: Quebec
Area: 1,540,680 sq km (594,861 sq miles)
Population: 6,540,000

SASKATCHEWAN
Capital: Regina
Area: 651,900 sq km (251,635 sq miles)
Population: 1,010,000

YUKON TERRITORY
Capital: Whitehorse
Area: 482,515 sq miles (186,250 sq miles)
Population: 24,000

Arctic hares

BAFFIN BAY

Inuit hunting for seals

Ringed seal

Narwhals

DAVIS STRAIT

Whistling swan

BAFFIN ISLAND

Lemmings

Canada goose

CANADA

Caribou

Inuit (Eskimos)

HUDSON STRAIT

Brent geese

Hooded seal

NEWFOUNDLAND

TORIES

Belugas (white whales)

Polar bear

HUDSON BAY

Wolverine

Furs

Iron ore

Porpoises

St. John's

Gannets

N   A   D   A

QUEBEC

Harp seals

Cod

Nickel

Black bear

Paper

PRINCE EDWARD ISLAND

CAPE BRETON ISLAND

Nelson

MANITOBA

Beaver

Timber

ONTARIO

PARLIAMENT BUILDINGS (OTTAWA)

NEW BRUNSWICK

Fredericton

NOVA SCOTIA

Halifax

LAKE WINNIPEG

Ice hockey

Sugar maple

CHÂTEAU FRONTENAC (QUEBEC)

Quebec

Copper

Iron and steel

CN TOWER (TORONTO)

OTTAWA

St Lawrence

Montreal

Scallops

Winnipeg

Grain storehouses

LAKE SUPERIOR

Cars

Toronto

ATLANTIC OCEAN

S   A

Hamilton

NIAGARA FALLS

LAKE ERIE

THE UNITED STATES

THE UNITED STATES OF AMERICA is one of the largest and richest countries in the world. It is made up of 50 states, each of which has its own government. The national government is based in the capital, Washington DC. The letters "DC" stand for District of Columbia, the name of the area in which the city is situated.

The country is dominated by two mountain ranges – the Rockies in the west and the Appalachians in the east. In between lie the flat, fertile Great Plains, which are used for farming. The United States is rich in natural resources. It has large deposits of raw materials, such as iron, coal, and oil, which are needed to produce industrial goods. These resources have helped the country to become the world's greatest industrial manufacturer. The United States is also rich in farmland, and exports large amounts of agricultural produce, especially cereals, cotton, and tobacco. Most years, the United States exports more grain than all the other countries of the world combined.

The United States is often described as a "melting pot" because its population is a mix of many peoples. The country's first inhabitants were the American Indians. Later, settlers came from all over Europe, especially the UK, Italy, Ireland, and Poland. The United States' black population are the descendants of slaves who were brought to America from Africa. More recent arrivals include Hispanics (Spanish-speakers) from Mexico and South America, and Asians.

FACTS AND FIGURES

The area of New England is famous for its spectacular forests and old wooden houses.

THE UNITED STATES
Capital: Washington DC
Area: 9,372,614 sq km (3,618,794 sq miles)
Population: 245,871,000
Language: English
Religion: Christian
Currency: US dollar
Government: Republic

THE NORTHEASTERN STATES

THE NORTHEASTERN part of the United States is the most crowded region in the country. Large numbers of people live along the Atlantic coast in the great cities of Boston, New York City, Philadelphia, Baltimore, and Washington. This coast was the first area of the United States to be settled by Europeans. In 1620 colonists from England, who are known as the "Pilgrim Fathers", established the first settlement at New Plymouth, Massachusetts, in the region that is still called New England.

Farther inland lie the Great Lakes, the largest group of freshwater lakes in the world, which form part of the border between the United States and Canada. The region around the Great Lakes has the greatest concentration of industry in the United States. The biggest cities are Chicago, Pittsburgh, and Detroit, which is known as the "Motor City" because it is the centre of the American car industry. The main products of the area are iron and steel, machinery, cars, chemicals, coal, and textiles.

West and southwest of the Great Lakes are the states of Minnesota, Wisconsin, and Iowa, which lie on the flat land of the Great Plains. Much of the United States' wheat and maize is grown in this area, which is often called the "farm belt".

New York City

The skyline of Manhattan Island in the centre of New York City is perhaps the best-known view of any city in the world. It was the first sight of America for the millions of people who emigrated there from Europe during the 19th and early 20th centuries. Today, New York is the largest city in the United States, the country's leading port, and a world financial centre.

Facts And Figures

The skyline of Chicago is dominated by the Sears Tower – the world's tallest building.

THE NORTHEASTERN STATES:

CONNECTICUT
Capital: Hartford
Area: 12,620 sq km (4,872 sq miles)
Population: 3,174,000

DELAWARE
Capital: Dover
Area: 5,005 sq km (1,932 sq miles)
Population: 622,000

ILLINOIS
Capital: Springfield
Area: 144,120 sq km (55,645 sq miles)
Population: 11,535,000

INDIANA
Capital: Indianapolis
Area: 93,065 sq km (35,932 sq miles)
Population: 5,499,000

IOWA
Capital: Des Moines
Area: 144,950 sq km (55,965 sq miles)
Population: 2,884,000

KENTUCKY
Capital: Frankfort
Area: 102,740 sq km (39,668 sq miles)
Population: 3,679,000

MAINE
Capital: Augusta
Area: 80,275 sq km (30,994 sq miles)
Population: 1,164,000

MARYLAND
Capital: Annapolis
Area: 25,480 sq km (9,837 sq miles)
Population: 4,392,000

MASSACHUSETTS
Capital: Boston
Area: 20,265 sq km (7,824 sq miles)
Population: 5,822,000

MICHIGAN
Capital: Lansing
Area: 147,520 sq km (56,957 sq miles)
Population: 9,088,000

MINNESOTA
Capital: St Paul
Area: 206,030 sq km (79,548 sq miles)
Population: 4,193,000

MISSOURI
Capital: Jefferson City
Area: 178,565 sq km (68,944 sq miles)
Population: 5,029,000

NEW HAMPSHIRE
Capital: Concord
Area: 23,290 sq km (8,992 sq miles)
Population: 998,000

NEW JERSEY
Capital: Trenton
Area: 19,340 sq km (7,467 sq miles)
Population: 7,562,000

NEW YORK
Capital: Albany
Area: 122,705 sq km (47,376 sq miles)
Population: 17,783,000

OHIO
Capital: Columbus
Area: 106,200 sq km (41,004 sq miles)
Population: 10,744,000

PENNSYLVANIA
Capital: Harrisburg
Area: 116,260 sq km (44,888 sq miles)
Population: 11,853,000

RHODE ISLAND
Capital: Providence
Area: 2,730 sq km (1,054 sq miles)
Population: 968,000

VERMONT
Capital: Montpelier
Area: 24,900 sq km (9,613 sq miles)
Population: 535,000

VIRGINIA
Capital: Richmond
Area: 102,835 sq km (39,695 sq miles)
Population: 5,387,000

WASHINGTON DC
Area: 163 sq km (63 sq miles)
Population: 626,000

WEST VIRGINIA
Capital: Charleston
Area: 62,470 sq km (24,119 sq miles)
Population: 1,936,000

WISCONSIN
Capital: Madison
Area: 140,965 sq km (54,427 sq miles)
Population: 4,775,000

500 Kilometres
300 Miles

C A N A D A

St Lawrence

White pine

Potatoes

Blueberries

M A I N E

VERMONT
Montpelier

Augusta

Skiing

FORT TICONDERAGA

NEW HAMPSHIRE

Concord

GULF OF MAINE

NEW YORK

Sugar maple

Boston

THE STATE HOUSE OF BOSTON

MASSACHUSETTS

CAPE COD

LAKE HURON

LAKE ONTARIO

Skiing

Albany

Hartford

CONNECTICUT

Providence

RHODE ISLAND

Cars

LAKE ST CLAIR

NIAGARA FALLS

THE STATUE OF LIBERTY

LONG ISLAND

Lansing
Detroit

LAKE ERIE

APPALACHIAN MTS

New York City

Tourism

Ocean liner

Cleveland

Akron

Oil

PENNSYLVANIA

Chemicals

Trenton

NEW JERSEY

Iron and steel

Iron and steel

Coal

Harrisburg

Soya beans

Tyres

Pittsburgh

Philadelphia

Tourism

O H I O

Columbus

Amish people

Baltimore

Dover

DELAWARE

Strip-mining coal

Annapolis

DELAWARE BAY

Baseball

Cincinnati

THE CAPITOL BUILDING

WASHINGTON DC

Ohio

WEST VIRGINIA

MARYLAND

Mackerel

Frankfort

Chemicals

Charleston

Richmond

Coal

V I R G I N I A

CHESAPEAKE BAY

Warship

KENTUCKY

THE NATURAL BRIDGE

Peanuts

A T L A N T I C   O C E A N

The Kentucky Derby

Tobacco

N O R T H   C A R O L I N A

SEE

THE SOUTHERN STATES

THE SOUTHERN STATES, which are often just called "the South", extend from the Atlantic coast in the east to the Mexican border in the west. Flowing southwards through the region is the Mississippi River, which reaches the Gulf of Mexico at New Orleans. Before the railways were built, the Mississippi was North America's most important trading route.

In the 18th and 19th centuries, the wealth of the South was based on farming. Cotton, tobacco, and other crops were grown on large farms called plantations. The workers on the plantations were black slaves, who were brought over from Africa. In the 1860s a civil war was fought in America between the southern states (the Confederacy) and the northern states (the Union). One of the main causes of the war was that the South refused to get rid of slavery. In 1865, the Union was victorious and the slaves were freed.

In the west of this region lies the huge state of Texas, which is famous for its cattle ranches and its oil. The long peninsula of Florida, in the southeast, is popular for holidays and attracts tourists from all over the world because of its good climate and beautiful beaches.

KANSAS

COLORADO

NEW MEXICO

OKLAHOMA

Arkansas

Natural gas

Wheat

Amarillo

Cotton

Armadillo

Dallas skyline

Diamonds

Lubbock

Rodeo

Helicopters

Fort Worth

Dallas

Red

American football

Shreveport

El Paso

Oil

Oil

Cotton

Electronics

Peanuts

Maize

Pecan nuts

Rio Grande

Waco

Brazos

Longhorn cattle

Pecos

Cowboy

Austin

THE ALAMO

Colorado

Petrochemicals

Rice

Houston

CHISOS MOUNTAINS

San Antonio

Oil

MEXICO

SAN JOSÉ MISSION

Oil

Corpus Christi

Brown pelicans

Citrus fruit

Oil

Shrimps

Rio Grande

GULF

| 0 | 100 | 200 | 300 | 400 Kilometres |
| 0 | 50 | 100 | 150 | 200 | 250 Miles |

NEW ORLEANS – THE CITY OF MARDI GRAS

New Orleans is the oldest city in the South. It was founded by the French in 1718, passed to the Spanish in 1763, and finally became part of America in 1803. The city's mixed history is reflected in its population, which includes large numbers of *creoles* (descendants of the early French and Spanish settlers) and blacks. Early each year, New Orleans holds its famous carnival, called the Mardi Gras. During the carnival the city is filled with spectacular street parades and the sound of jazz bands.

13 14 15 16 17 18 19 20 21 22 23

ILLINOIS INDIANA WEST VIRGINIA VIRGINIA

ISSOURI KENTUCKY

Soya beans
Country and western music
Poultry *Textiles* *Tobacco*
First powered flight by the Wright brothers

Nashville **Knoxville** **Greensboro** **Raleigh**

Catfish

TENNESSEE **APPALACHIAN MTS** **NORTH CAROLINA**

Cotton *Dairy cattle*
Memphis **Chattanooga** *Tennessee* *Black bear* **Charlotte** *Sweet potatoes*

ARKANSAS
Little Rock
Rice *Coca Cola* *Textiles*
Oil **SOUTH**
Magnolia tree **Columbia** *Tobacco* **CAROLINA**
Mississippi steamer *Iron and steel* **Atlanta** **Charleston** *Shrimps*
Coca Cola **CONFEDERATE MEMORIAL (STONE MT)** *Savannah*

MISSISSIPPI **ALABAMA** **GEORGIA**
Birmingham *Soya beans*
Cotton **Columbus** *Cotton* **Savannah**
Montgomery *Alabama* *Cotton* *Paper* *Yellowtail snapper*
Jackson *Raccoon* *Peanuts* *Flint* *Water melons*
Jazz music *Pearl* *Oil* *Palmetto tree*
LOUISIANA *Oil* **Mobile** *Chattahoochee* **Jacksonville** *Tourism*
Oil **Baton Rouge** *Apalachicola* **Tallahassee** **FLORIDA**
Alligator **New Orleans** *Shrimps* *Cruiser*
MISSISSIPPI DELTA
Oil rig *Oysters* *Lobster*

THE EPCOT CENTRE (DISNEY WORLD) **Orlando** **CAPE CANAVERAL (SPACE LAUNCH SITE)**
Tampa

THE EVERGLADES *Tourism* **BAHAMAS**
Fort Lauderdale
Miami
Anhinga (diving bird)

FLORIDA KEYS

GULF OF MEXICO

ATLANTIC OCEAN

A C D E F G H K L M N O

FACTS AND FIGURES

The city of Miami in Florida is a popular tourist resort. Many Americans retire there.

Largest cities: Dallas-Fort Worth (Texas), 3,725,000; Houston (Texas), 3,626,000; Miami (Florida), 2,954,000; Atlanta (Georgia), 2,657,000; New Orleans (Louisiana), 1,257,000.

Longest river: Mississippi, 3,778 km (2,348 miles).

World's largest theme park: Disney World, in Florida, covers an area of 113 sq km (44 sq miles). It had over 22 million visitors in 1988.

THE SOUTHERN STATES:

ALABAMA
Capital: Montgomery
Area: 131,485 sq km (50,766 sq miles)
Population: 4,021,000

ARKANSAS
Capital: Little Rock
Area: 134,880 sq km (52,077 sq miles)
Population: 2,359,000

FLORIDA
Capital: Tallahassee
Area: 140,255 sq km (54,152 sq miles)
Population: 11,366,000

GEORGIA
Capital: Atlanta
Area: 150,365 sq km (58,056 sq miles)
Population: 5,976,000

LOUISIANA
Capital: Baton Rouge
Area: 115,310 sq km (44,521 sq miles)
Population: 4,481,000

MISSISSIPPI
Capital: Jackson
Area: 122,335 sq km (47,233 sq miles)
Population: 2,613,000

NORTH CAROLINA
Capital: Raleigh
Area: 126,505 sq km (48,843 sq miles)
Population: 6,255,000

SOUTH CAROLINA
Capital: Columbia
Area: 78,225 sq km (30,202 sq miles)
Population: 3,347,000

TENNESSEE
Capital: Nashville
Area: 106,590 sq km (41,154 sq miles)
Population: 4,762,000

TEXAS
Capital: Austin
Area: 678,620 sq km (262,017 sq miles)
Population: 16,370,000

The state of Texas is famous for its huge cattle ranches, where cowboys still round up the animals on horseback.

THE WESTERN STATES

THE WESTERN part of the United States has the most rugged landscape in the country, with high mountains, deserts, and river canyons. The Rocky Mountains, which dominate the states of Idaho, Montana, Wyoming, and Colorado, mark where the West begins. The early settlers struggled across this difficult countryside in their wagon trains, but it was not until the railways were built during the mid-1800s that the American West was opened up.

California is situated on the Pacific coast and has the largest population of any of the American states. The first Europeans to settle there were the Spanish, as can be seen from many of the place names, such as Los Angeles, San Francisco and San Diego. The central valley of California contains some of the richest farming land in the country. California lies on the San Andreas Fault, where two parts of the Earth's crust are slowly moving in different directions. This movement causes frequent earthquakes.

SAN FRANCISCO – THE CITY ON THE BAY

The city of San Francisco grew rapidly during the California Gold Rush of 1849, when miners flooded into California in search of their fortunes. In 1906 San Francisco was struck by an earthquake and large parts of the city were destroyed. Modern San Francisco is built on the hills around the bay.

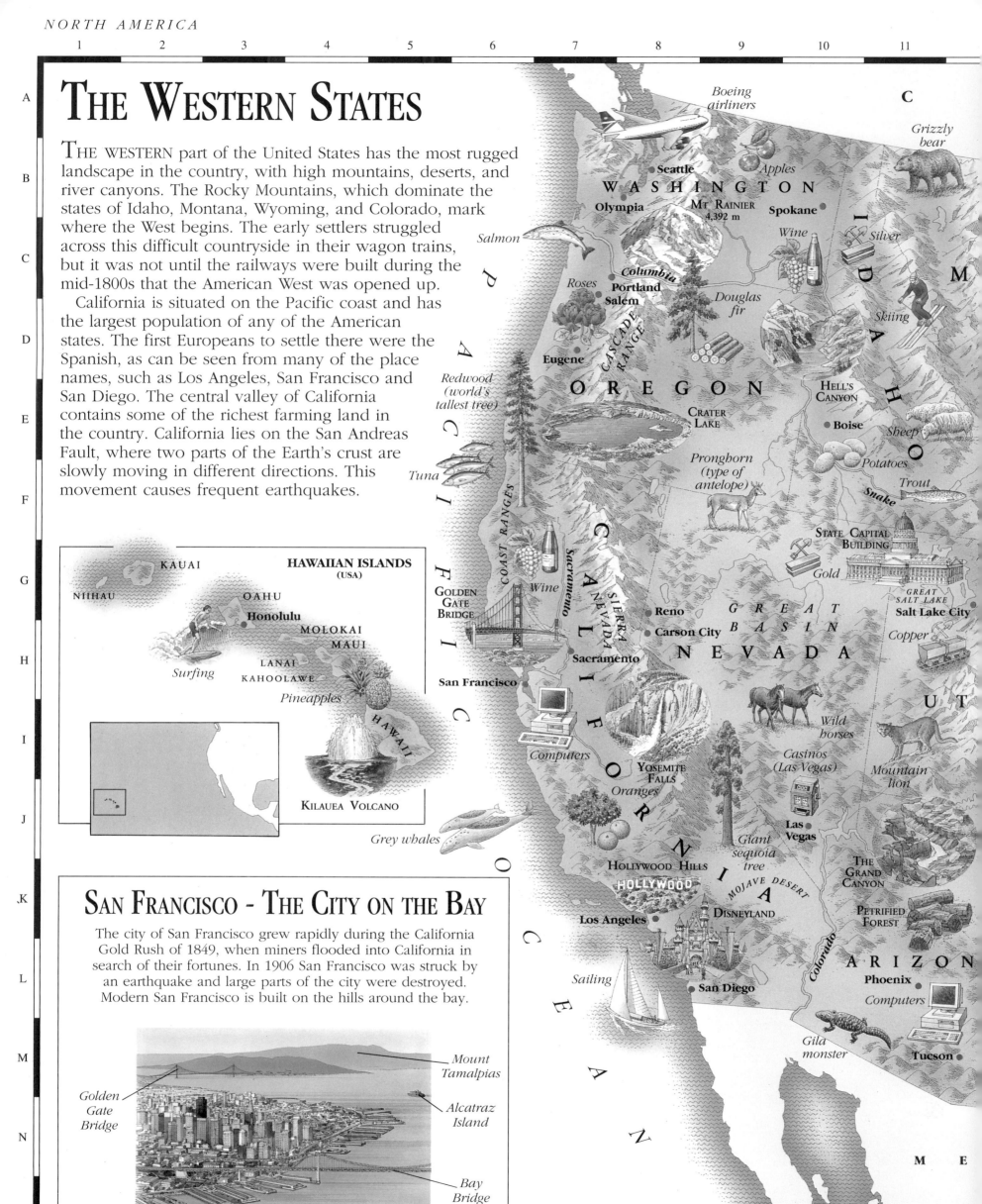

HAWAIIAN ISLANDS
(USA)

KAUAI
NI'IHAU
OAHU
Honolulu
MOLOKAI
MAUI
LANAI
KAHOOLAWE
Surfing
Pineapples
HAWAII
KILAUEA VOLCANO

Golden Gate Bridge
Mount Tamalpias
Alcatraz Island
Bay Bridge

WASHINGTON
Seattle
Olympia
Mt Rainier 4,392 m
Spokane
Apples
Wine
Boeing airliners
Grizzly bear
IDAHO
Silver
Skiing
Salmon
Columbia
Portland
Salem
Roses
CASCADE RANGE
Douglas fir
OREGON
Eugene
HELL'S CANYON
Boise
Sheep
Potatoes
Trout
Snake
CRATER LAKE
Redwood (world's tallest tree)
Tuna
Pronghorn (type of antelope)
STATE CAPITAL BUILDING
Gold
GREAT SALT LAKE
Salt Lake City
Copper
COAST RANGES
Wine
Sacramento
SIERRA NEVADA
GOLDEN GATE BRIDGE
San Francisco
Reno
Carson City
GREAT BASIN
NEVADA
UTAH
CALIFORNIA
Computers
YOSEMITE FALLS
Oranges
Wild horses
Casinos (Las Vegas)
Mountain lion
Giant sequoia tree
Las Vegas
THE GRAND CANYON
Grey whales
Hollywood Hills
HOLLYWOOD
MOJAVE DESERT
PETRIFIED FOREST
Los Angeles
DISNEYLAND
Colorado
ARIZONA
Phoenix
Computers
Sailing
San Diego
Gila monster
Tucson
PACIFIC OCEAN
MEXICO

A N A D A

Harvesting wheat

Oil

Oil

Wild ducks

Great Falls

Missouri

Grand Forks

N O R T H

M O N T A N A

Oil

D A K O T A

Helena

Oil

Bismarck

Wheat

M I N N E S O T A

Old Faithful Geyser (Yellowstone National Park)

Yellowstone

DEVIL'S TOWER

Strip-mining for coal!

Missouri

Sunflowers

S O U T H

D A K O T A

Wapiti (type of elk)

Pierre

Beef cattle

R O C K Y

Gannett Peak 4,207 m

Beef cattle

I O W A

Prairie dog

Missouri

W Y O M I N G

MT RUSHMORE

Soya beans

Coyote (type of wild dog)

N E B R A S K A

Cowboy

Cheyenne

Wheat

Omaha

Missouri

CHIMNEY ROCK

Lincoln

Skiing

Colorado

Denver

Denver skyline

BUFFALO BILL'S RANCH HOUSE

Kansas City

M I S S O U R I

C O L O R A D O

Topeka

RAINBOW BRIDGE

K A N S A S

Aircraft industry

Oil

Topeka

SHIP ROCK

Indian eagle dancer

MONUMENT ROCKS

Wichita

Sorghum (cereal crop)

M I S S I S S I P P I

Rattlesnake

Oil

Tulsa

A R K A N S A S

Beef cattle

Oil

Santa Fe

Cotton

Oklahoma City

Albuquerque

N E W M E X I C O

Bison

O K L A H O M A

Saguaros (giant cacti)

SOCORRO SPACE TELESCOPE

Maize

SAN XAVIER DE BAC MISSION

Rio Grande

CARLSBAD CAVERNS

T E X A S

M E X I C O

Scale: 0 100 200 300 400 500 Kilometres
0 100 200 300 Miles

FACTS AND FIGURES

The city of Las Vegas in Nevada is famous for its nightclubs and gambling casinos.

THE WESTERN STATES:

ARIZONA
Capital: Phoenix
Area: 293,985 sq km (113,508 sq miles)
Population: 3,489,000

CALIFORNIA
Capital: Sacramento
Area: 404,815 sq km (156,300 sq miles)
Population: 28,314,000

COLORADO
Capital: Denver
Area: 268,310 sq km (103,595 sq miles)
Population: 3,301,000

HAWAII
Capital: Honolulu
Area: 16,640 sq km (6,425 sq miles)
Population: 1,098,000

IDAHO
Capital: Boise
Area: 213,455 sq km (82,415 sq miles)
Population: 1,003,000

KANSAS
Capital: Topeka
Area: 211,805 sq km (81,778 sq miles)
Population: 2,495,000

MONTANA
Capital: Helena
Area: 376,555 sq km (145,389 sq miles)
Population: 805,000

NEBRASKA
Capital: Lincoln
Area: 198,505 sq km (76,643 sq miles)
Population: 1,602,000

NEVADA
Capital: Carson City
Area: 294,625 sq km (113,755 sq miles)
Population: 1,054,000

NEW MEXICO
Capital: Santa Fe
Area: 314,255 sq km (121,334 sq miles)
Population: 1,507,000

NORTH DAKOTA
Capital: Bismarck
Area: 179,485 sq km (69,300 sq miles)
Population: 667,000

OKLAHOMA
Capital: Oklahoma City
Area: 177,815 sq km (68,635 sq miles)
Population: 3,242,000

OREGON
Capital: Salem
Area: 249,115 sq km (96,184 sq miles)
Population: 2,767,000

SOUTH DAKOTA
Capital: Pierre
Area: 196,715 sq km (75,952 sq miles)
Population: 713,000

UTAH
Capital: Salt Lake City
Area: 212,570 sq km (82,074 sq miles)
Population: 1,690,000

WASHINGTON
Capital: Olympia
Area: 172,265 sq km (66,512 sq miles)
Population: 4,648,000

WYOMING
Capital: Cheyenne
Area: 251,200 sq km (96,989 sq miles)
Population: 479,000

MEXICO, CENTRAL AMERICA, AND THE CARIBBEAN

CENTRAL AMERICA is a narrow land bridge that joins the two continents of North and South America. At its narrowest point, in Panama, a canal 82 km (51 miles) long has been built to join the Atlantic and Pacific oceans. There are seven small countries in Central America. To the north lies Mexico and to the east lie the hundreds of islands of the Caribbean Sea, which are often called the West Indies. This is a region of great variety and contrasts – large and small, rich and poor, old and new – with a fascinating mixture of different cultures and troubled histories. Modern Mexico City, the largest city in the world, lies on the site of an ancient city called Tenochtitlán, which was once the capital of the Aztec civilization.

On the Caribbean islands, tourist luxury and local poverty lie side by side. In the 16th century, the islands were colonized by the Europeans, who shipped black slaves from Africa to work on the farms. Today the population is a mixture of many peoples. The main languages are English, Spanish, and dialects called *patois*, which are mixtures of African and French or English.

There are also great contrasts in the climate and vegetation of this area, from the Mexican desert in the north to the rainforests of the south, and the clear blue waters and coral islands in the east. Sometimes great tropical storms called hurricanes rage through the usually calm waters of the Caribbean. Winds of over 160 kph (100 mph) and enormous waves cause much damage.

TEOTIHUACÁN

Teotihuacán, located near modern Mexico City, was the capital city of an ancient Mexican civilization. Its name means "the city of the gods". At the height of its importance, around AD 600, it had 125,000 inhabitants and covered an area of more than 20 sq km (8 sq miles). The streets were laid out in a grid pattern and were lined with temples, palaces and about 20,000 houses. The huge Pyramid of the Sun, in the middle of the city, was one of the earliest religious centres in Mexico. In about AD 750 the city was destroyed by invaders and abandoned.

13　14　15　16　17　18　19　20　21　22　23

FACTS AND FIGURES

Jamaica, which means "island of springs", is a popular tourist resort.

World's fastest population growth: The population of Central America has more than tripled since 1900.

ANTIGUA & BARBUDA
Capital: St John's

ARUBA
Capital: Oranjestad

BAHAMAS
Capital: Nassau

BARBADOS
Capital: Bridgetown

BELIZE
Capital: Belmopan

COSTA RICA
Capital: San José

CUBA
Capital: Havana

DOMINICA
Capital: Roseau

DOMINICAN REPUBLIC
Capital: Santo Domingo

EL SALVADOR
Capital: San Salvador

GRENADA
Capital: St George's

GUADELOUPE
Capital: Basse Terre

GUATEMALA
Capital: Guatemala City

HAITI
Capital: Port-au-Prince

HONDURAS
Capital: Tegucigalpa

JAMAICA
Capital: Kingston

MARTINIQUE
Capital: Fort-de-France

MEXICO
Capital: Mexico City

NETHERLANDS ANTILLES
Capital: Willemstad

NICARAGUA
Capital: Managua

PANAMA
Capital: Panama City

PUERTO RICO
Capital: San Juan

ST KITTS-NEVIS
Capital: Basseterre

ST LUCIA
Capital: Castries

ST VINCENT & THE GRENADINES
Capital: Kingstown

TRINIDAD & TOBAGO
Capital: Port-of-Spain

ATLANTIC OCEAN

U S A

M E X I C O

Flags:
BAHAMAS　PUERTO RICO　BARBADOS　GRENADA　TRINIDAD & TOBAGO
CUBA　JAMAICA　HAITI　DOMINICAN REPUBLIC

Tourism

BAHAMAS
NASSAU

Cruise liner

Scuba diver

STRAITS OF FLORIDA

Sugar cane

Coral reefs

TURKS & CAICOS ISLANDS (UK)

Cocoa

Coral reefs

Frigate bird

Tourism

ANGUILLA (UK)

VIRGIN ISLANDS (USA/UK)

ST KITTS-NEVIS

ANTIGUA & BARBUDA

Coffee

HAVANA

C U B A

Pineapples

Coffee

HAITI

DOMINICAN REPUBLIC

SANTO DOMINGO

PORT-au-PRINCE

PUERTO RICO (US)

SAN JUAN

MONTSERRAT (UK)

GUADELOUPE (Fr)

Coconuts

Sailing

DOMINICA

MARTINIQUE (Fr)

Cigars

Scuba diver

CAYMAN ISLANDS (UK)

JAMAICA

KINGSTON

Reggae music　*Rum*

Sharks

ST LUCIA

BARBADOS

ST VINCENT & THE GRENADINES

Nutmeg and mace

GRENADA

Steel bands

Green turtle

C A R I B B E A N　S E A

Grapefruit

HONDURAS

Cattle

TEGUCIGALPA

Coffee

Bananas

NICARAGUA

MANAGUA

Coffee

Toucan

SAN JOSÉ

COSTA RICA

P A N A M A

PANAMA CANAL

PANAMA CITY

Spider monkey

TRINIDAD & TOBAGO

ARUBA (Neth)

NETHERLANDS ANTILLES

C O L O M B I A

V E N E Z U E L A

0　200　400　600　800 Kilometres
0　100　200　300　400　500 Miles

13　14　15　16　17　18　19　20　21　22　23

SOUTH AMERICA

THE CONTINENT of South America is made up of great mountain ranges, thick forests, wide plains, and deserts. Running from north to south down the western side of South America are the snow-capped peaks of the Andes. These mountains are amongst the most recently formed on Earth and in places they are still slowly rising. Along the range of mountains are hundreds of volcanoes, some of which are still active. Many of the streams and rivers which join together to form the mighty Amazon river start in the Andes. The Amazon basin, which lies across the Equator, is a hot, wet region which contains the largest tropical rainforest in the world.

The flat, fertile grasslands of the Pampas in the southeast of the continent are used for rearing cattle on huge farms called ranches, and for growing wheat. Farther south lies the colder, desert landscape of Patagonia. At the tip of the continent is Cape Horn, for centuries feared by sailors because fierce storms rage there for much of the year.

Ancient Inca city at Machu Picchu, Peru.

Saw mill on the Amazon River.

In 1498 Christopher Columbus became the first European to see the coast of South America. Europeans quickly colonized the continent, and until the beginning of the 19th century South America was ruled by Spain and Portugal. Argentina was the first country to gain its independence, in 1816. The people of South America are descended from American Indians, Europeans, and Africans. Spanish is the main language, except in Brazil, where Portuguese is spoken. Many Indians speak their own languages.

About half of South America's people make their living from farming. Most farmers grow just enough beans or corn for their families to live on, but there are large plantations where coffee, sugar-cane, wheat, and other crops are grown. South America is also rich in natural resources, such as oil, gold, silver, copper, iron, tin, and lead.

Peruvians in national costume.

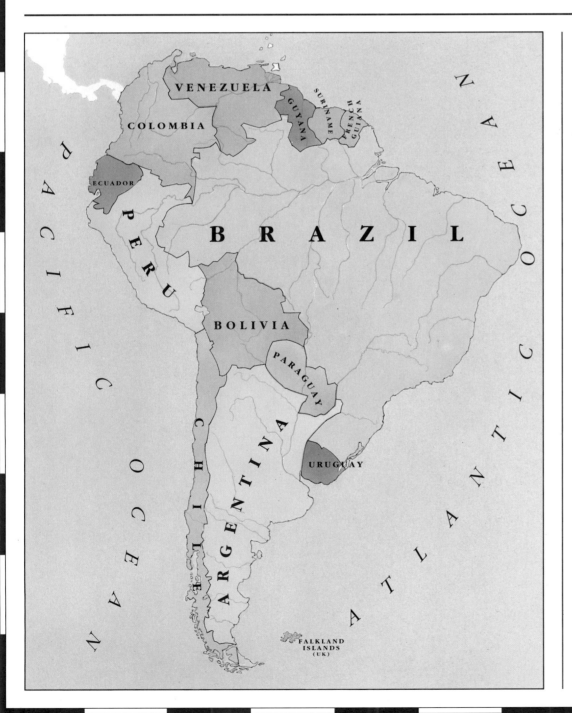

P

FACTS ABOUT SOUTH AMERICA

Area: 17,835,000 sq km (6,886,000 sq miles).

Population: 283,519,000.

Number of independent countries: 12.

Largest countries: Brazil, 8,511,965 sq km (3,286,726 sq miles); Argentina, 2,776,889 sq km (1,068,304 sq miles).

Most populated countries: Brazil, 144,369,000; Argentina, 31,506,000.

Largest cities: São Paulo (Brazil), 15,784,000; Rio de Janeiro (Brazil), 10,489,000; Buenos Aires (Argentina), 9,968,000.

Highest mountains: Aconcagua (Argentina), 6,960 m (22,834 ft), the world's highest extinct volcano; Ojos del Salado (Argentina-Chile), 6,908 m (22,664 ft), the world's highest active volcano; Bonete (Argentina), 6,872 m (22,546 ft).

Longest rivers: Amazon, 6,437 km (4,000 miles); Paraná, 4,500 km (2,796 miles); Madeira, 3,199 km (1,988 miles); São Francisco, 3,199 km (1,988 miles); Tocantins, 2,639 km (1,640 miles).

Main deserts: Atacama (Chile), about 80,290 sq km (31,000 sq miles); Patagonia (Argentina), about 770,000 sq km (300,000 sq miles).

Largest forest area: Amazon basin, about 7,000,000 sq km (2,700,000 sq miles).

Largest lake: Lake Titicaca (Peru-Bolivia), 8,340 sq km (3,220 sq miles). Titicaca is also the highest navigable lake in the world.

Largest island: Tierra del Fuego (Chile-Argentina), 47,000 sq km (18,140 sq miles).

World's wettest place: Tutunendo (Colombia) has an average annual rainfall of 11,770 mm (463.4 in).

World's driest place: Parts of the Atacama Desert (Chile) have an average annual rainfall of nil. In 1971 rain fell there for the first time in over 400 years.

World's highest waterfall: Angel Falls on the River Carrao (Venezuela) has a total drop of 979 m (3,212 ft).

World's largest lagoon: Lagoa dos Patos (Brazil) covers 10,645 sq km (4,110 sq miles).

NORTH AMERICA

ATLANTIC

A

B

C

D

GULF OF MEXICO

GREATER ANTILLES

LESSER ANTILLES

CARIBBEAN SEA

CENTRAL AMERICA

AFRICA

LAKE MARACAIBO

Orinoco

GULF OF PANAMA

GUIANA HIGHLANDS

MARAJO ISLAND

GALAPAGOS ISLANDS

Negro

Amazon

AMAZON

BASIN

Madeira

Tocantins

Parnaíba

A N D E S

MATO

GROSSO

São Francisco

BRAZILIAN

HIGHLANDS

△ Mt Huascarán
6,768 m

LAKE TITICACA

GRAN CHACO

Paraguay

Paraná

TRINIDADE

LAKE POOPO

ATACAMA DESERT

OJOS DEL SALADO
6,908 m
△ BONETE 6,872 m

Paraná

Uruguay

LAGOA DOS PATOS

△ Mt Aconcagua
6,960 m

PACIFIC

OCEAN

PAMPAS

RÍO DE LA PLATA

PATAGONIA

BAHIA BLANCA

GULF OF ST MATIAS

TRISTAN DA CUNHA

L

FALKLAND ISLANDS
(ISLAS MALVINAS)

SOUTH GEORGIA ISLAND

M

TIERRA DEL FUEGO

CAPE HORN

DRAKE PASSAGE

SOUTH SHETLAND ISLANDS

SOUTH SANDWICH ISLANDS

N

ATLANTIC

OCEAN

O

A N T A R C T I C A

NORTHERN SOUTH AMERICA

THE NORTHERN PART of South America is dominated by the vast, humid Amazon rainforest and by the high, snow-capped Andes mountains in the west. The Amazon river is the second longest in the world, after the Nile, and runs for 6,437 km (4,000 miles) from its source in the Peruvian Andes to its mouth in northern Brazil. Every hour the Amazon delivers an average of 773 billion litres (170 billion gallons) of water into the Atlantic.

The Andes region of Peru was the centre of the great Inca empire, which flourished in the 15th and 16th centuries. It was destroyed in 1532-33 by the Spanish conquistadors, led by Francisco Pizarro. The Incas were brilliant engineers, building roads and canals through difficult mountain landscapes. They were also skilled scientists, craftsmen, and farmers.

Brazil is by far the largest country in South America, both in size and population. In the over-crowded cities of southeast Brazil, such as São Paulo and Rio de Janeiro, large numbers of poor people live in slums known as "favelas".

In recent years, political and social problems have caused much upheaval in this region. Some of the nations are ruled by dictators. Colombia is one of the most dangerous countries in the world because of its ruthless drug trade. Tourism, however, remains an important source of income in South America.

COLUMBIA

ECUADOR

HUASCARÁN 6,768 m △

PERU

BOLIVIA

Map labels

Scarlet Ibis
Pearls
Barranquilla
Cartagena
Oil
Oil
CARACAS
Valencia
Barquisimeto
Oil
Oil
Ciudad Bolívar
PANAMA
Emeralds
VENEZUELA
Diamonds
BOGOTÁ CATHEDRAL
Medellín
Orinoco
Manizales
BOGOTÁ
Harpy eagle
COLOMBIA
ANGEL FALLS
Cali
Red howler monkey
Bananas
Coffee
Jaguar
Negro
Panama hat
Pre-Columbian stone idol
Capybara (world's largest rodent)
Quito
△ COTOPAXI 5,897 m
ECUADOR
Peruvian cock-of-the-rock
Indian hunter
Coffee
Iquitos
Cavies (guinea pigs)
Humming bird
Piura
Indian flute players
Toco toucan
Rainforest
Chiclayo
Llama
Madeira
Trujillo
Rubber trees
Pôrto Velho
ANDES MTS
PERU
MACHU PICCHU (INCA CITY)
Two-toed sloth
LIMA
Spectacled bear
PACIFIC
PERU
LAKE TITICACA
La Paz
△ ILLIMANI 6,882 m
Andean condor
Arequipa
BOLIVIA
Cochabamba
Santa Cruz
Sucre
Reed boat on Lake Titicaca
BOLIVIA
Bolivian Indian
Puya raimandii (world's tallest herb)
OCEAN

THE AMAZON RAINFOREST

The Amazon rainforest covers an area larger than Western Europe and supports more than one-fifth of the world's plant and animal species. It is also the home of tribes of Indians who have lived there for thousands of years. But each year about 200,000 sq km (77,200 sq miles) of forest is cut down for farming and mining. As a result of deforestation, many of the plants and animals are disappearing.

GALÁPAGOS ISLANDS
(ECUADOR)

Marine iguana
Galápagos giant tortoise
ISABELA ISLAND

0   50   100 Kilometres
0   25   50   75 Miles

VENEZUELA

GUYANA

SURINAME

FRENCH GUIANA

0   200   400   600   800   1000 Kilometres
0   150   300   450   600 Miles

A T L A N T I C

O C E A N

GUYANA

Georgetown

Paramaribo

Sugar cane

Cayenne

SURINAME

FRENCH GUIANA

ARIANE ROCKET LAUNCH SITE

Wayana Indian

Green turtle

Lobster

BRAZIL

Jangada fishing raft

MANAUS OPERA HOUSE

Water buffalo

Gold and blue macaw

Manaus

Amazon

MARAJÓ ISLAND

Belém

Coconut palms

Mango tree

Anaconda

Gold

Xingu

Caiman

Kayapo Indian

Brazil nuts

Fortaleza

Tourism

Teresina

Bananas

Natal

Suya Indian

Umbrella bird

Tapir

CHURCH OF OUR LADY OF CARMO

Recife

B   R   A   Z   I   L

Araguaia

Tocantins

São Francisco

Marmoset

Giant armadillo

BRASILIA CATHEDRAL DOME

Tourism

Sugar cane

Cuiabá

M A T O G R O S S O

Salvador

Cocoa pods

Cattle

Brasília

Gold

Shrimps

Campo Grande

Coffee

Football

Tourism

Humming bird

Belo Horizonte

CORCOVADO STATUE OF CHRIST

Jabiru stork

Carnival

Campinas

Rio de Janeiro

Wheat

SUGAR LOAF MT 395 m

Gaucho (cattleherder)

Curitiba

Cars

Tourism

São Paulo

Paraná

Hake

PORTO ALEGRE CATHEDRAL

Porto Alegre

Soya beans

FACTS AND FIGURES

Traditional reed boats are still used on Lake Titicaca, the highest navigable lake in the world.

Highest mountains:
Huascarán (Peru), 6,768 m (22,205 ft); Illimani (Bolivia), 6,882 m (22,579 ft).

Longest rivers:
Amazon, 6,437 km (4,000 miles); Madeira, 3,199 km (1,988 miles); São Francisco, 3,199 km (1,988 miles); Tocantins, 2,639 km (1,640 miles).

Largest lake: Lake Titicaca (Peru-Bolivia), 8,340 sq km (3,220 sq miles).

World's biggest waterfall: Angel Falls (Venezuela), 979 m (3,212 ft).

Largest cities:
São Paulo (Brazil), 15,784,000; Rio de Janeiro (Brazil), 10,489,000; Lima (Peru), 5,494,000.

World's leading coffee grower: Brazil grows around 4,000,000 tonnes (3,936,826 tons) of coffee each year.

Sugar Loaf Mountain stands at the entrance to the harbour in Rio de Janeiro, one of Brazil's major ports.

BOLIVIA
Capital: La Paz
Area: 1,098,581 sq km (424,195 sq miles)
Population: 6,917,000

BRAZIL
Capital: Brasília
Area: 8,511,965 sq km (3,286,726 sq miles)
Population: 144,369,000

COLOMBIA
Capital: Bogotá
Area: 1,138,914 sq km (439,770 sq miles)
Population: 30,007,000

ECUADOR
Capital: Quito
Area: 283,561 sq km (109,526 sq miles)
Population: 10,154,000

FRENCH GUIANA
Capital: Cayenne
Area: 90,000 sq km (34,751 sq miles)
Population: 90,000

GUYANA
Capital: Georgetown
Area: 214,969 sq km (82,980 sq miles)
Population: 799,000

PERU
Capital: Lima
Area: 1,285,216 sq km (496,260 sq miles)
Population: 20,681,000

SURINAME
Capital: Paramaribo
Area: 163,265 sq km (63,041 sq miles)
Population: 429,000

VENEZUELA
Capital: Caracas
Area: 912,050 sq km (352,170 sq miles)
Population: 18,759,000

SOUTHERN SOUTH AMERICA

THE TWO LARGEST COUNTRIES in southern South America are Argentina and Chile. Their people are mainly of European descent. The landscape in Argentina varies dramatically, from the Andes mountains to forests, grassy plains and the bare, windswept plateau of Patagonia. The country is rich in mineral deposits, such as oil, natural gas, coal, and iron ore, but its most important natural resource is the Pampas – a fertile, grassy plain where large numbers of cattle are reared. Argentina is one of the world's main exporters of beef.

Chile is a long, thin strip of land stretching about 4,200 km (2,610 miles) from Peru to Punta Arenas, the southern-most city in the world. Separated from the rest of South America by the Andes, Chile has many kinds of climate, from the Atacama Desert in the north, to ice and glaciers in the south. Chile has huge deposits of minerals, such as copper, iron ore and nitrates, which account for much of its wealth.

In the countries of Paraguay and Uruguay most people make their living from agriculture, especially raising sheep and cattle. Paraguay is among the world's poorer countries – most farmers there grow just enough to support their families.

The Falkland Islands, which are governed by the United Kingdom, lie in the Atlantic Ocean about 500 km (310 miles) off the coast of Argentina. They are surrounded by rich fishing grounds and oil reserves. The islands are also claimed by the Argentinians, who call them the *Islas Malvinas*. Most people in the Falkland Islands make their living from sheep farming.

PARAGUAY

ARGENTINA

CHILE

URUGUAY

BRAZIL

BOLIVIA

PERU

PARAGUAY

GRAN CHACO

ARGENTINA

PAMPAS

CHILE

ANDES

ATACAMA DESERT

Paraguay

Concepción

Asunción

Corrientes

Resistencia

Santiago del Estero

San Miguel de Tucumán

Córdoba

Santa Fe

Rosario

Buenos Aires

La Plata

Montevideo

San Juan

Mendoza

Mr Aconcagua 6,960 m

Santiago

Viña del Mar

Valparaíso

Rancagua

Arica

Iquique

Antofagasta

Paraná

Paraguay

Paraná

Uruguay

Salado

Atuel

Ojos del Salado 6,908 m

Licancabur Volcano 5,921 m

Iguassu Falls

Oranges

Tobacco

Cotton

Cotton

Cotton

Maté (type of tea)

Carreta (ox-drawn cart)

Cattle

Cattle

Cattle

Cattle

Cattle

Quebracho tree

Football

Polo players

Rhea

Wine

Wine

Wine

Wine

Skiing

Cherries

Andean condor

Giant anteater

Prickly pear

Vicuña (type of llama)

Alpaca

Copper

Iron

Sugar cane

Gaucho (cattleherder)

Gaucho (cattleherder)

Tango dancers

Colon Opera House

Sheep

Río de la Plata

Tourism

THE ANDES

The Andes are the longest mountain chain in the world. They stretch 7,240 km (4,500 miles), from the Caribbean Sea in the north to Cape Horn in the south. The Andes are among the most recently formed mountains on Earth, and frequent volcanic eruptions and earthquakes show that the Earth's crust is still moving in this area.

FALKLAND ISLANDS
(UK)

STANLEY
Albatross
Sheep
Rock bopper penguins

Mar del Plata
Dusky dolphins
Tourism
Bahía Blanca
Wheat
Right whale

ATLANTIC OCEAN

Colorado
Negro
Colorado
Sheep
Mara (type of guinea pig)
Maned wolf
Chubut
Chico
Oil
Comodoro Rivadavia
Magellan penguins
Sealions

Asado (Argentinian barbecue)
Hairy armadillo
Chubut
Darwin's rhea
Guanacos (llama)
Sheep

PATAGONIA

Skiing
Timber
Timber
Morèno Glacier
Río Gallegos
Sheep
Oil
Oil
Punta Arenas
Oil
Oil
Ushuaia
TIERRA DEL FUEGO
CAPE HORN

Huaso (Chilean cowboy)
Trout
Salmon
Fur seals

Concepción
E
Mackerel
Fishing boats

PACIFIC OCEAN

STRAIT OF MAGELLAN

FACTS AND FIGURES

Gauchos are South American cowboys who herd cattle on the large ranches of the Pampas.

ARGENTINA
Capital: Buenos Aires
Area: 2,766,889 sq km (1,068,304 sq miles)
Population: 31,506,000
Language: Spanish
Religion: Christian

CHILE
Capital: Santiago
Area: 756,945 sq km (292,259 sq miles)
Population: 12,760,000
Language: Spanish
Religion: Christian

FALKLAND ISLANDS (ISLAS MALVINAS)
Capital: Stanley
Area: 12,170 sq km (4,699 sq miles)
Population: 2,000
Language: English
Religion: Christian

PARAGUAY
Capital: Asunción
Area: 406,752 sq km (157,048 sq miles)
Population: 4,042,000
Languages: Spanish, Guaraní
Religion: Christian

URUGUAY
Capital: Montevideo
Area: 177,414 sq km (68,500 sq miles)
Population: 3,004,000
Language: Spanish
Religion: Christian

Parinacota, near Lake Chungara in Chile, is one of the many active volcanoes in the Andes.

Highest mountains:
Mt Aconcagua (Argentina-Chile), 6,960 m (22,834 ft); Ojos del Salado (Argentina Chile), 6,908 m (22,664 ft).

Longest river: Paraná, 4,500 km (2,796 miles).

Largest cities: Buenos Aires (Argentina), 9,968,000; Santiago (Chile), 4,858,000; Montevideo (Uruguay), 1,246,000; Córdoba (Argentina), 982,000; Rosario (Argentina), 955,000; Asunción (Paraguay), 729,000.

Largest island: Tierra del Fuego, 47,000 sq km (18,140 sq miles).

No rain has fallen in parts of the Atacama Desert in Chile for over 400 years.

800 Kilometres
500 Miles
600
400
200
300
400
200
100
0
0

EUROPE

The headquarters of the EC in Brussels, Belgium.

EUROPE IS THE SECOND smallest continent by area, but it has the second largest population of all the six continents. Europe is bounded by the Atlantic and Arctic Oceans in the north and west, and in the south by the Mediterranean Sea. Europe's only land frontier – with Asia – is marked by the Ural Mountains in the USSR.

The landscape of Europe is very varied. In southern Europe, much of the land is hilly or mountainous. The history of this region has been greatly influenced by the Mediterranean Sea, which for centuries has been a vital trade route between Europe, Africa, and Asia.

The northern and southern parts of mainland Europe are divided by the Alps, the highest range of mountains in western Europe. The landscape of northern Europe is generally flat and is dominated by the North European Plain, which stretches from the Atlantic coast right across to the Ural Mountains. In the far north of the continent lie the mainly mountainous countries of Scandinavia.

Since the end of the Second World War in 1945, the European countries have been divided into two groups – the West and the East. The border between the West and the East was called the Iron Curtain, because few people were allowed to cross it.

The Eastern European countries are Romania, Poland, Yugoslavia Czechoslovakia, Hungary, Bulgaria, Albania, and the area that was formerly East Germany. Until the late 1980s, these countries had communist governments, and many of them were closely linked to the USSR. But

Vegetable market in Montenegro, Yugoslavia.

in recent years, some of the Eastern European countries have broken away from communist control and relations between the East and the West have improved dramatically.

The Western European countries differ in many ways, but they have in common that their governments are chosen by the people in free elections. The Western European nations are among the richest countries in the world.

Twelve countries in Western Europe have joined together to form the European Community (EC), sometimes called the Common Market. The member states are Belgium, Denmark, France, Germany, Greece, Ireland, Italy, Luxembourg, the Netherlands, Portugal, Spain, and the UK. The aim of the EC is to unite the economic resources of its members into a single economy. In the future, there may also be a form of political union between the EC countries.

During the 18th and 19th centuries Western European countries became the first nations in the world to go through an industrial revolution. Instead of getting most of their wealth from farming, they changed to manufacturing and exporting industrial goods. Although today Europe still has the greatest concentration of industry of all the continents, a large number of Europeans still make their living from farming.

Lavender fields in France.

FACTS ABOUT EUROPE

Area: 10,498,000 sq km (4,053,309 sq miles). This is seven per cent of the world's total land area.

Population: 690,000,000 (including the European part of the USSR). This is nearly 14 per cent of the world's total population.

Number of countries: 33 (this includes 3 per cent of Turkey and 25 per cent of the USSR).

Largest countries: USSR - the European part of the USSR covers 5,571,000 sq km (2,151,000 sq miles), this is only 25 per cent of the total area of the USSR; France, 551,500 sq km (212,936 sq miles).

Most populated countries: USSR - 188,912,000 people live in the European part of the USSR; Germany, 77,714,000.

Largest cities: Moscow (USSR), 8,967,000; Paris (France), 8,707,000; London (UK), 6,735,000; Leningrad (USSR), 5,020,000; Berlin (Germany), 3,300,000.

Highest mountains: Elbrus (USSR), 5,642 m (18,510 ft); Mont Blanc (France-Italy), 4,807 m (15,770 ft); Monte Rosa (Italy-Switzerland), 4,634 m (15,203ft).

Longest rivers: Volga, 3,531 km (2,194 miles); Danube, 2,858 km (1,776 miles); Dnieper, 2,201 km (1,368 miles).

ICELAND

NORWEGIAN SEA

NORWAY

SWEDEN

FINLAND

ATLANTIC OCEAN

IRELAND

UNITED KINGDOM

DENMARK

NETHERLANDS

BELGIUM

LUXEMBOURG

GERMANY

POLAND

U S S R

(EUROPE)   (ASIA)

FRANCE

SWITZERLAND

AUSTRIA

CZECHOSLOVAKIA

HUNGARY

ROMANIA

CASPIAN SEA

ITALY

YUGOSLAVIA

BULGARIA

BLACK SEA

PORTUGAL

SPAIN

ALBANIA

TURKEY

GREECE

MALTA

MEDITERRANEAN SEA

A T L A N T I C

NORTH AMERICA

ARCTIC
OCEAN

GREENLAND

ZEMLYA
FRANTSA-IOSIFA

SVALBARD

NOVAYA ZEMLYA

BARENTS
SEA

NORWEGIAN
SEA

ICELAND

FAEROE
ISLANDS

KJÖLEN MTS

LAKE
ONEGA

LAKE
LADOGA

URAL MTS

BRITISH
ISLES

NORTH
SEA

BALTIC SEA

Elbe

Rhine

CENTRAL
RUSSIAN
UPLANDS

A S I A

AZORES

BAY OF
BISCAY

NORTH EUROPEAN PLAIN

Dnieper

Don

Volga

CASPIAN SEA

Rhone

ALPS

Po

CARPATHIANS

PYRENEES

Tagus

APENNINES

HUNGARIAN
PLAIN

Danube

CAUCASUS

MADEIRA

CORSICA

BLACK SEA

CANARY
ISLANDS

BALEARIC
ISLANDS

SARDINIA

MEDITERRANEAN

SICILY

CRETE

CYPRUS

SEA

ARABIAN
PENINSULA

AFRICA

RED SEA

OCEAN

INDIAN OCEAN

A
B
C
D

L
M
N
O

THE BRITISH ISLES

THE BRITISH ISLES lie off the northwestern coast of mainland Europe. They consist of two large islands – Great Britain and Ireland – surrounded by many smaller ones. The British Isles are divided into two countries: the United Kingdom and Ireland. The United Kingdom, which is often known as Britain, is itself made up of England, Wales, Scotland, and Northern Ireland.

During the 18th and 19th centuries, the United Kingdom was the first country in the world to undergo an industrial revolution. It became the world's leading manufacturing and trading nation. During this period, Britain acquired an enormous empire, covering more than a quarter of the world. Britain's colonies included Canada, Australia, New Zealand, India, and much of Africa. During the 20th century, almost all of these colonies have become independent, although they remain linked with Britain through the Commonwealth, which has 50 member countries. Today, the United Kingdom is a member of the European Community.

Until this century, Ireland was part of the United Kingdom. In 1921 the southern part of Ireland became an independent country. Most people in the south are Roman Catholic. The northern part of Ireland, where the people are mainly Protestant, remained part of the United Kingdom. The division of Ireland has caused the violent clashes which have taken place in Northern Ireland in recent years.

UNITED KINGDOM

SHETLAND ISLANDS

Lerwick

Crofting (farming)

Pilchard

Seals

Cod

ORKNEY ISLANDS

Haddock

Fish packing

Aberdeen

Highland dress

Oil rig

Fishing trawler

Whisky

BALMORAL CASTLE

BEN NEVIS 1343 m

Machinery

Edinburgh

EDINBURGH CASTLE

HADRIAN'S WALL

Newcastle upon Tyne

Chemicals

Carlisle

THE LOCH NESS MONSTER

LOCH LOMOND

SCOTLAND

Glasgow

Golf

Sheep

Shipbuilding

Red deer

Sheep

LEWIS

Salmon

SKYE

MULL

Highland cattle

ARRAN

ISLAY

GIANT'S CAUSEWAY

Londonderry

LOUGH NEAGH

NORTHERN IRELAND

Belfast

Textiles

HEBRIDES

NORTH UIST

SOUTH UIST

Making Harris tweed

ATLANTIC OCEAN

NORTH SEA

Fish packing

Castle Howard
Middlesbrough
PENNINES
Hull
Humber Bridge
Tourism
Fish packing
Wheat
Norwich
Fish packing
Ipswich
Oysters
Lavenham Guildhall
Cambridge
St Paul's Cathedral
Southend
Thames
Dover
Fruit
Cricket
Trent
Cars
Nottingham
Coventry
ENGLAND
Stratford-upon-Avon
Shakespeare's Birthplace
Oxford
Oxford student
Reading
LONDON
Brighton Pavilion and Pier
Cross-channel ferry
FRANCE

Coal
Sheffield
Leeds
Bradford
Iron and steel
Textiles
Manchester
China
Stoke-on-Trent
Electronics
Birmingham
Chemicals
Severn
Southampton
Machinery
Stonehenge
Portsmouth
Isle of Wight
Sailing

Liverpool
Football
SNOWDON △ 1,085 m
Sheep
THE BRECON BEACONS
Cardiff
Bristol
Salisbury Cathedral
Bournemouth
Tourism
ENGLISH CHANNEL

Blackpool
Tourism
Isle of Man
Douglas
Motorbike racing
IRISH SEA
Ferry
ANGLESEY
Welsh national costume
WALES
Swansea
Iron and steel
BRISTOL CHANNEL
Exeter
Tourism
Sailing
Mackerel
CHANNEL ISLANDS

Plaice
ST GEORGE'S CHANNEL
Puffins
Pollack
Dairy cattle
Plymouth
Warship
China clay
GOONHILLY EARTH-TRACKING DISH
ISLES OF SCILLY

CELTIC SEA

Customs House (Dublin)
DUBLIN
Guinness
Crystal
Sailing
River Cruising
Waterford
Cashel Monastery
Cork
IRELAND
Shannon
Limerick
Dairy cattle
CARRAUNTOOHIL 1,038 m
Petrochemicals

Potatoes
Horses
Lobster

IRELAND

LONDON

London, the capital city of the United Kingdom, was founded by the Romans. London contains many famous historic buildings and is the country's centre of politics, administration, law and culture. The square mile known as the City of London is one of the world's most important financial centres.

Royal Academy
Piccadilly Circus
Trafalgar Square
Cleopatra's Needle
Hayward Gallery
Houses of Parliament
Buckingham Palace
St James's Palace
Westminster Abbey

150 Kilometres
100 Miles

FRANCE

FRANCE is one of Europe's major farming and industrial nations and is famous for the food and wine it produces. The landscape in France varies dramatically from region to region and includes rich farmland, hot, dry areas, snow-capped mountains, and large forests.

France has always been an important European power. In 1789 the French over-threw their king, Louis XVI, during the French Revolution. After the revolution, Napoleon, a general in the French army, seized power and crowned himself Emperor. He went on to conquer most of mainland Europe, but was defeated at the Battle of Waterloo in 1815. During the 19th century, French explorers and soldiers won a large colonial empire in Africa and Asia.

Today France is one of the world's leading manufacturing countries, with large iron, steel, chemical, car, aeroplane, and textile industries. France is also rich in farming land. Its major crops include barley, oats, wheat, flax, sugar beet, and grapes. Dairy farming is widespread and French farmers produce over 700 different types of cheese.

Tourism is another important source of wealth. There are many resorts around the coasts of France, and the Alps and Pyrenees are popular for winter sports.

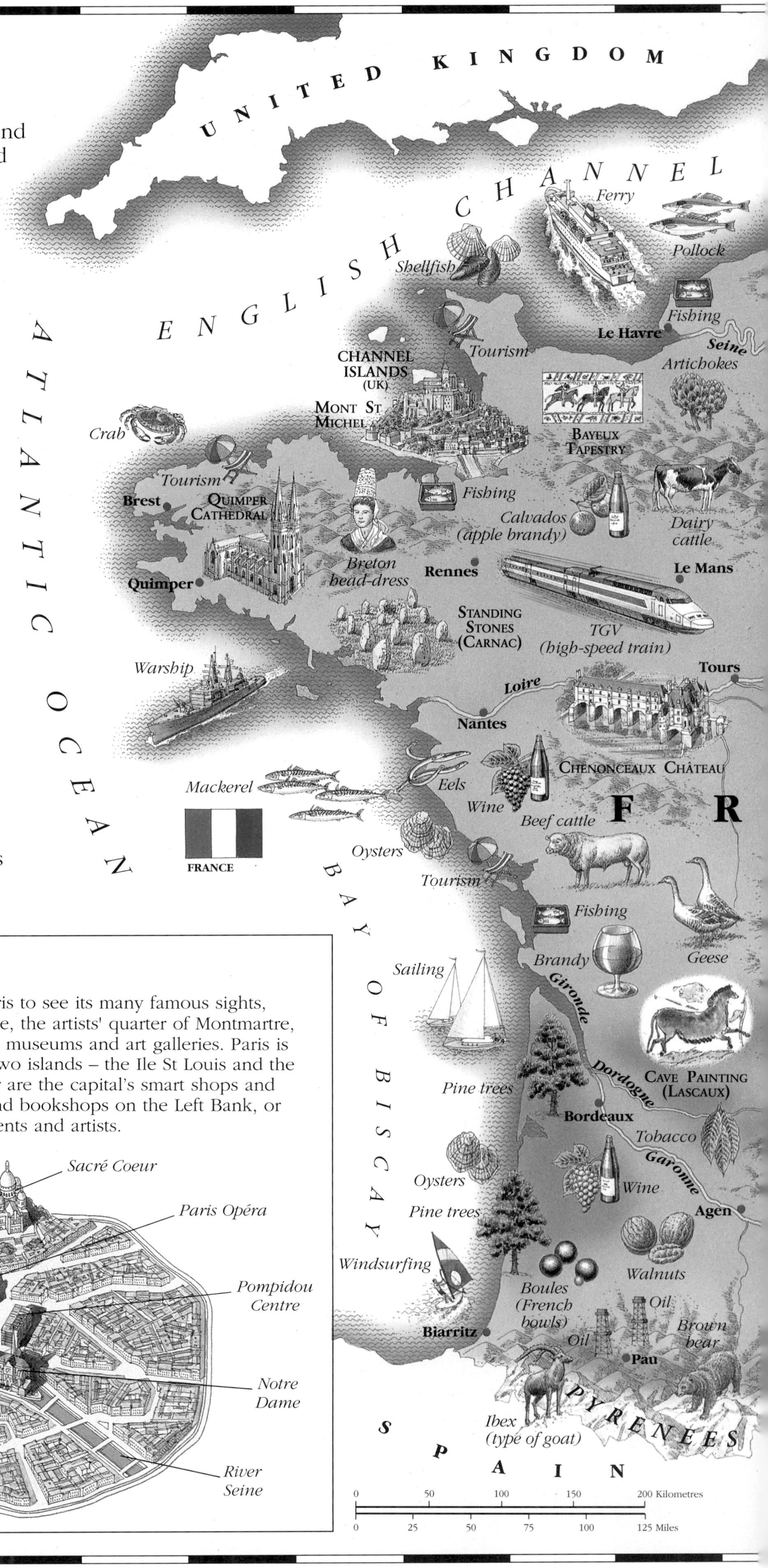

PARIS

Visitors from all over the world flock to Paris to see its many famous sights, including the Eiffel Tower, the Arc de Triomphe, the artists' quarter of Montmartre, the tree-lined avenues, or *boulevards,* and the museums and art galleries. Paris is built on both sides of the River Seine and on two islands – the Ile St Louis and the Ile de la Cité. On the Right Bank of the river are the capital's smart shops and fashion houses. The many pavement cafés and bookshops on the Left Bank, or Latin Quarter, attract students and artists.

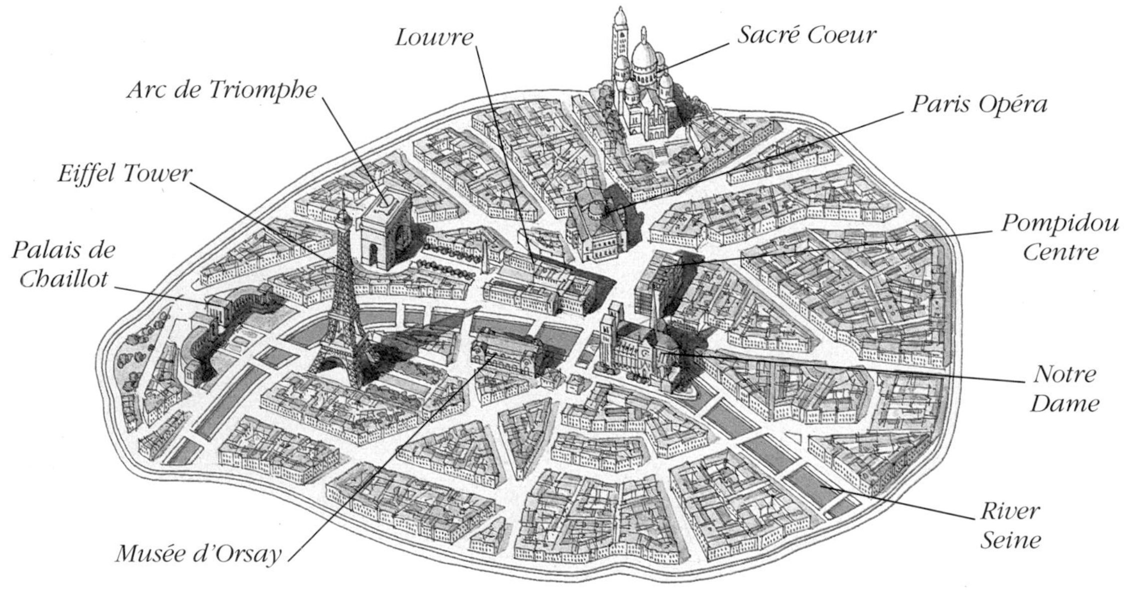

Paris map labels:
- Arc de Triomphe
- Louvre
- Sacré Coeur
- Paris Opéra
- Eiffel Tower
- Palais de Chaillot
- Pompidou Centre
- Notre Dame
- Musée d'Orsay
- River Seine

Map labels:
UNITED KINGDOM
ENGLISH CHANNEL
ATLANTIC OCEAN
BAY OF BISCAY
Ferry
Shellfish
Pollock
Le Havre
Seine
Fishing
Artichokes
CHANNEL ISLANDS (UK)
Tourism
MONT ST MICHEL
BAYEUX TAPESTRY
Crab
Tourism
Fishing
Calvados (apple brandy)
Dairy cattle
Brest
QUIMPER CATHEDRAL
Breton head-dress
Rennes
Le Mans
Quimper
STANDING STONES (CARNAC)
TGV (high-speed train)
Tours
Warship
Loire
Nantes
CHENONCEAUX CHÂTEAU
Mackerel
Eels
Wine
Beef cattle
F R
FRANCE
Oysters
Tourism
Fishing
Brandy
Geese
Sailing
Gironde
CAVE PAINTING (LASCAUX)
Pine trees
Dordogne
Bordeaux
Tobacco
Oysters
Garonne
Pine trees
Wine
Agen
Windsurfing
Walnuts
Boules (French bowls)
Oil
Biarritz
Oil
Brown bear
Pau
Ibex (type of goat)
SPAIN
PYRENEES

Scale: 0 50 100 150 200 Kilometres
0 25 50 75 100 125 Miles

Map labels

BELGIUM
GERMANY
LUXEMBOURG
SWITZERLAND
ITALY

Calais
Dunkerque
Lille
Tourism
Somme
WORLD WAR I MEMORIAL (VIMY)
Amiens
AMIENS CATHEDRAL
Beef cattle
Fashion design
Cars
PIERREFONDS CHÂTEAU
PARIS
CHÂTEAU BAS (SEDAN)
Coal
Coal
Wine
Reims
Metz
Champagne
Potatoes
Nancy
Strasbourg
Pigs
Storks
Wheat
Seine
Wild boar
CHARTRES CATHEDRAL
Orléans
Loire
SAINTE MADELEINE (VÉZELAY)
Mustard
Mulhouse
CHAPEL OF NOTRE DAME DU HAUT
Wine
Dijon
CHAMBORD CHÂTEAU
CHÂTEAUNEUF (NIEVRE)
Beaune
Wine
Saône
Deer
FRANCE
Mâcon
TGV (high-speed train)
Porcelain
Wine
MONT BLANC 4,807 m
Limoges
Clermont-Ferrand
Lyon
St Etienne
Rhône
Hunting for truffles
MASSIF CENTRAL
Skiing
Cycling
Grenoble
Mountain climbing
CHAPEL OF ST MICHEL D'AIGUILHE (LE PUY)
CEVENNES
ALPS
Rhône
Wine
Chamois (type of goat)
Snails
Sheep
PONT VALENTRE (CAHORS)
Olives
Aircraft industry
Tourism
M O N A C O
Montpellier
Nice
Cannes
AMPHITHEATRE AT ARLES
Lavender
Tourism
Garonne
Toulouse
Marseille
Toulon
WALLED TOWN (CARCASSONNE)
Flamingos
Fishing
Sailing
Warship
Tourism
SOLAR FURNACE (ODEILLO)
Wine
Sardines
M E D I T E R R A N E A N
S E A

MONACO

CORSICA (FRANCE)
Bastia
CORSICA
Tourism
Ajaccio
Tourism
Tourism

Facts and Figures sidebar

FACTS AND FIGURES

Amboise is one of the many historic towns along the River Loire in eastern France.

Highest mountains:
Mont Blanc, 4,807 m (15,770 ft);
Les Ecrins, 4,103m (13,461 ft); Pic
de Vignemale, 3,298 m (10,820 ft);
Mont Dore, 1,886 m (6,188 ft).

Longest rivers:
Loire, 1,005 km (625 miles);
Rhône-Saône, 812 km (505 miles);
Seine, 775 km (481 miles).

Largest cities:
Paris, 8,707,000; Lyon, 1,221,000;
Marseille, 1,111,000; Lille, 936,000;
Bordeaux, 640,000.

The TGV, which runs between Paris and Lyon, is one of the world's fastest trains, with a top speed of 270 kph (168 mph).

F R A N C E
Capital: Paris
Area: 551,500 sq km (212,936 sq miles)
Population: 55,873,000
Language: French
Religion: Christian
Currency: French franc

M O N A C O
Capital: Monaco
Area: 1.6 sq km (0.6 sq miles)
Population: 29,000
Language: French
Religion: Christian
Currency: French franc

Sunflowers are grown all over southern France. Their seeds are used to make cooking oil.

BELGIUM, THE NETHERLANDS, AND LUXEMBOURG

BELGIUM, THE NETHERLANDS, AND LUXEMBOURG are situated on the North European Plain, where much of the land is very flat and low lying. For this reason, they are often called the "Low Countries". The only area of higher land in the region is the hilly Ardennes forest in southern Belgium and Luxembourg.

Almost half of the Netherlands lies below sea level. There is a saying that "God made the world, but the Dutch made the Netherlands", because over the centuries the Dutch have reclaimed large areas of land from the sea. The reclaimed land, called a polder, is drained and then protected against flooding with long walls called dykes.

Belgium, the Netherlands, and Luxembourg are sometimes called "Benelux", which is a shortened version of the three country names. Although these countries are small, they have large populations. The Netherlands has one of the highest concentrations of people in Europe – an average of 360 people live in each square kilometre of land. All three Benelux countries have successful industrial economies. Farming is also important, and the most up-to-date methods are used. The main products are livestock, dairy produce, fruit, vegetables, and flowers. Fishing and tourism are also important sources of income. Belgium and the Netherlands have been important trading nations for many centuries. Today, Rotterdam in the Netherlands and Antwerp in Belgium are the two busiest ports in Europe.

The Benelux countries are members of the European Community, which has its headquarters in Brussels, the Belgian capital. Luxembourg is a centre for European organizations, while the International Courts of Justice are situated at The Hague in the Netherlands.

THE NETHERLANDS

Windmill
Gas
MARTINI TOWER (GRONINGEN)
Groningen
Potatoes
Sugar beet
Cattle
Wooden clogs
HUNEBEDS (PREHISTORIC MONUMENTS)
Beef cattle
Zwolle
Ijssel
Leeuwarden
Ice skating
Yachting
Wheat
Bulbs
Canal-side houses
Cyclists
Hengelo
Enschede
Horses
Apeldoorn
Arnhem
Rhine
Fruit
Nijmegen
Maas (Meuse)
Venlo
Asparagus
Traditional Dutch costume
UTRECHT CATHEDRAL TOWER
Hilversum
's-HERTOGENBOSCH CATHEDRAL
Tilburg
Eindhoven
Electronics
Pigs
Wheat
Utrecht
Lek
Waal
Cheese porters
Alkmaar
Edam cheese
Haarlem
AMSTERDAM
Bulbs
Diamond cutting
Leiden
Vegetables
Rotterdam
Dordrecht
Windmill
Breda
ANTWERP CATHEDRAL
Antwerp
Cyclist
Tourism
THE HAGUE
Delft pottery
Container terminal (Rotterdam)
PORT OF ANTWERP
Schelde
Herrings
Dam (sea barrier)
Plaice
Ferry
MAISON DES FRANC BATELIERS (GHENT)
Ghent
BRUGES TOWN HALL
Bruges
Ostend
Lace-making
Tourism
Shrimps
Sheep
Avocet
Terns
WEST FRISIAN ISLANDS
WADDENZEE
IJSSELMEER

THE NETHERLANDS

Map labels

R E G I E

Chemicals

Maastricht

Iron and steel

Mt BOTRANGE 694 m

Wild boar

BELGIUM

LUXEMBOURG

Liège

Apples

Louvain TOWN HALL

Crystal

Meuse

A R D E N N E S

Deer

CLERVAUX

Wine

LUXEMBOURG

LUXEMBOURG

Esch-sur-Alzette

THE ARDENNES FOREST

WALZIN

Namur

Brussels

Chocolates

EC HEADQUARTERS

B E L G I U M

Vegetables

Oudenaarde

Kortrijk

TOURNAI CATHEDRAL

Tournai

Beef cattle

Cattle

Beer

Mons

Iron and steel

Charleroi

Sambre

Pigs

F R A N C E

The National Monument

The Royal Palace   Nieuwe Kerk

Dam Square

AMSTERDAM

Amsterdam, the largest city in the Netherlands, is named after a dam which was built on the River Amstel in the 13th century. Like much of the country, Amsterdam lies below sea level. Large parts of the city are built on huge wooden or concrete piles sunk deep into the soggy ground. A network of canals more than 80 km (50 miles long) criss-crosses the city and helps to drain the land.

By the end of the 16th century, Amsterdam had become the leading port in the Netherlands. For the next hundred years it was also Europe's most important port and trading centre and specialized in trade with the Far East. Many of the famous buildings in the city centre, such as the Royal Palace and the Stock Exchange, date from this period.

Today Amsterdam is a major commercial and financial centre. Many of its industries, such as processing tobacco, coffee, tea and other imported goods, diamond cutting, and shipbuilding, have developed from its historical trading connections.

FACTS AND FIGURES

BELGIUM

Capital: Brussels
Area: 30,514 sq km (11,781 sq miles)
Population 9,867,000
Languages: French, Flemish, some German
Religion: Christian
Currency: Belgian franc

LUXEMBOURG

Capital: Luxembourg
Area: 2,586 sq km (998 sq miles)
Population: 371,000
Languages: Luxembourgish, French, German
Religion: Christian
Currencies: Luxembourg franc, Belgian franc

THE NETHERLANDS

National capital: Amsterdam
Seat of government: The Hague
Area: 40,844 sq km (15,770 sq miles)
Population: 14,760,000
Language: Dutch
Religion: Christian
Currency: Guilder

The historic city of Bruges in Belgium is the centre of the country's lace-making industry.

Highest mountain: Mt Botrange (Belgium), 694 m (2,277 ft).

Lowest point: Prins Alexander Polder (Netherlands), 6.7 m (22 ft) below sea level.

Largest cities: Rotterdam (Netherlands),1,040,000; Amsterdam (Netherlands), 1,038,000; Brussels (Belgium), 970,000; The Hague (Netherlands), 683,000.

Every two years a festival of flowers takes place in the Grande Place in the centre of Brussels in Belgium.

Rotterdam in the Netherlands is the world's largest port. It has 122 km (76 miles) of quayside.

80 Kilometres
50 Miles

A

SCANDINAVIA

SCANDINAVIA consists of the four countries of Denmark, Norway, Sweden, and Finland, which are situated in northern Europe, and the island of Iceland, which lies in the North Atlantic Ocean.

The landscape of Scandinavia varies from country to country. Denmark is low lying, and much of the land is used for farming. In contrast, almost all of Norway is mountainous, and the country's coastline is dotted with long, narrow bays called fjords. Finland is a land of forests and lakes, while Sweden has an extremely varied landscape, which includes forest, farmland, mountains

and lakes. The central part of Iceland is a plateau of volcanoes, lava fields and glaciers, so most of the people live around the coast. The people of Scandinavia are the descendants of the Vikings, who lived there about 1,000 years ago. The Vikings are usually remembered as warriors and seafarers, but for most of the time they lived peacefully as farmers and fishermen.

Scandinavia has important natural resources, including the timber in its large forests, fish in the surrounding seas, iron ore in northern Sweden, and oil and natural gas in the North Sea off the coast of Norway. Today, the Scandinavian countries all have successful industrial economies, and their people enjoy a high standard of living.

THE FJORDS

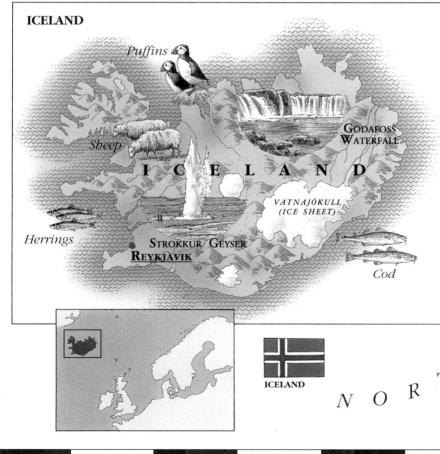

During the last great Ice Age, huge ice sheets and glaciers formed over Scandinavia. The moving ice carved out deep, steep-sided valleys. When the ice sheets began to melt, about 11,000 years ago, many of these valleys were filled by the sea, forming the famous Norwegian fjords.

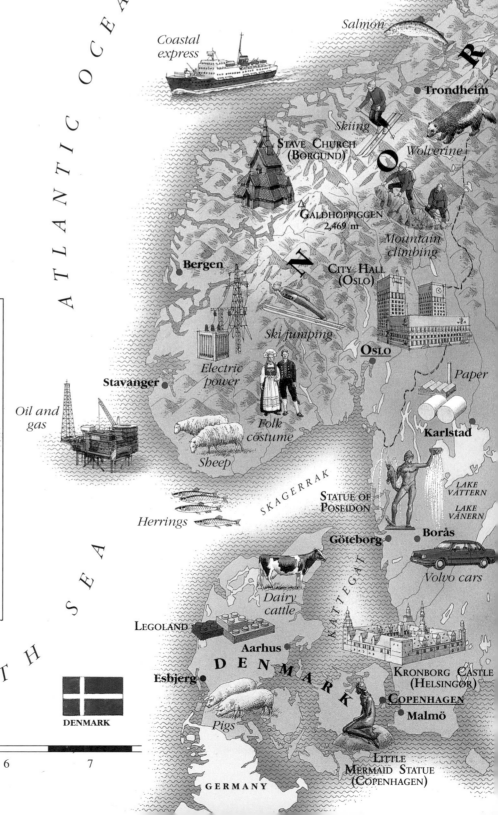

NORWEGIAN SEA

Fishing trawler

NORWAY

ATLANTIC OCEAN

Coastal express

Salmon

Trondheim

Skiing

STAVE CHURCH (BORGUND)

Wolverine

Bergen

GALDHØPIGGEN 2,469 m

Mountain climbing

CITY HALL (OSLO)

Ski jumping

Oslo

Electric power

Paper

Stavanger

Folk costume

Oil and gas

Sheep

Karlstad

Herrings

SKAGERRAK

LAKE VÄTTERN

Statue of Poseidon

LAKE VÄNERN

Göteborg

Borås

Dairy cattle

Volvo cars

LEGOLAND

Aarhus

DENMARK

KRONBORG CASTLE (HELSINGØR)

Esbjerg

COPENHAGEN

Malmö

Pigs

GERMANY

LITTLE MERMAID STATUE (COPENHAGEN)

ICELAND

Puffins

GODAFOSS WATERFALL

Sheep

ICELAND

VATNAJÖKULL (ICE SHEET)

Herrings

STROKKUR GEYSER

REYKJAVIK

Cod

ICELAND

NORTH SEA

DENMARK

NORTH CAPE

B A R E N T S
S E A

Fishing trawler

Reindeer

Tromsø

VESTERÅLEN

Cod

LOFOTEN
ISLANDS

Puffins

Narvik

Sami
(Lapps)

Wolves

L A P L A N D

K
J
Ö
L
E
N
M
T
S

Iron ore

S
W
E
D
E
N

Birch tree

F
I
N
L
A
N
D

Salmon

Elk

Lynx

Norway spruce

Cross-country skiing

Sailing

Furs

Sauna

Oulu

Scots pine

G
U
L
F
O
F
B
O
T
H
N
I
A

Umeå

Salmon

Herrings

Paper

Folk costume

Model horse
(Dalarna)

TAMPERE
CATHEDRAL

Trout

F
I
N
L
A
N
D

Tampere

DROTTINGHOLM
PALACE

Potatoes

Lahti

HELSINKI
RAILWAY
STATION

Turku

Uppsala

ÅLAND
ISLANDS

HELSINKI

Örebro

STOCKHOLM

Ice-breaker
ship

CITY HALL
(STOCKHOLM)

GULF OF FINLAND

R
U
S
S

Rune stone
(ancient
inscription)

GOTLAND

B
A
L
T
I
C
S
E
A

ÖLAND

Guillemots

FACTS AND FIGURES

Scandinavia's large forests are an important source of wealth. Much of the timber is used to make paper.

Highest mountain:
Galdhøppiggen (Norway),
2,469 m (8,100 ft).

Largest lake: Lake Vänern
(Sweden), 5,580 sq km (2,155 sq miles).

Largest cities:
Stockholm (Sweden), 1,617,000;
Copenhagen (Denmark),
1,339,000; Helsinki (Finland),
987,000; Oslo (Norway), 456,000;
Göteborg (Sweden), 431,000.

FINLAND

The city of Copenhagen in Denmark has been an important port and trading centre since the Middle Ages.

DENMARK
Capital: Copenhagen
Area: 43,077 sq km (16,632 sq miles)
Population: 5,133,000
Language: Danish
Religion: Christian
Currency: Danish krone
Government: Monarchy

FINLAND
Capital: Helsinki
Area: 338,127 sq km (130,551 sq miles)
Population: 4,944,000
Languages: Finnish, Swedish
Religion: Christian
Currency: Markka
Government: Republic

ICELAND
Capital: Reykjavik
Area: 103,000 sq km (39,768 sq miles)
Population: 249,000
Language: Icelandic
Religion: Christian
Currency: Icelandic krona
Government: Republic

NORWAY
Capital: Oslo
Area: 323,895 sq km (125,056 sq miles)
Population: 4,205,000
Languages: Norwegian, Lappish
Religion: Christian
Currency: Norwegian krone
Government: Monarchy

SWEDEN
Capital: Stockholm
Area: 440,945 sq km (170,250 sq miles)
Population: 8,357,000
Language: Swedish
Religion: Christian
Currency: Swedish krona
Government: Monarchy

In central Iceland, volcanoes and hot water springs lie next to frozen rivers of ice, called glaciers.

SWEDEN

0   50   100   150   200   250 Kilometres

0   50   100   150 Miles

GERMANY, AUSTRIA, AND SWITZERLAND

THE LANDSCAPE in this region varies greatly, changing from flat plains in the north to high mountains in the south. It is crossed by two of Europe's longest rivers: the Rhine, which flows northwards to the North Sea, and the Danube, which flows eastwards to the Black Sea.

For hundreds of years, the area now called Germany consisted of many small independent states. These states were first united to form a single country in 1871. Germany rapidly became an important industrial and political power. In this century, Germany was defeated in two world wars. After World War II the country was split into two parts: the Federal Republic of Germany (West Germany) and the communist German Democratic Republic (East Germany). This split lasted for over 40 years. During this period relations between the two countries were often hostile because of their different political systems. The two German states were reunited in 1990, following the collapse of the communist government in East Germany. Today, Germany is amongst the world's most successful industrial nations and is the wealthiest country in Europe.

South of Germany lie the mountainous countries of Austria and Switzerland. Tourism, particularly winter sports, is an important source of wealth for both these countries. Switzerland is famous for its watches and scientific instruments, and is also a major banking and business centre. The country has been neutral since 1815 and has stayed out of all the wars that have affected Europe since that time. Austria is also neutral. The tiny country of Liechtenstein, which lies between Switzerland and Austria, is only about 24 km (15 miles) long and 8 km (5 miles) wide.

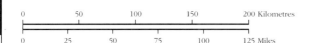

THE ALPS

EIGER 3,970 m   MÖNCH 4,099 m   JUNGFRAU 4,158 m

The Alps are the longest and highest mountain range in western Europe. They stretch from southeastern France, through Italy, Switzerland, and Austria, into northern Yugoslavia – a distance of about 1,200 km (750 miles). People from around the world visit the Alps to take part in sports such as skiing and mountaineering.

13   14   15   16   17   18   19   20   21   22   23

BALTIC SEA

RÜGEN

Shipbuilding

Rostock

Storks

Sheep

Schwerin

Sugar beet

Dairy cattle

P O L A N D

BRANDENBURG GATE

Machinery **Berlin**

Potsdam

Magdeburg

Pigs

Poultry

Halle

Elbe

Leipzig

ZWINGER PALACE

Strip-mining coal

Iron and steel

Textiles

Chemnitz

Zwickau

Dresden

Y

FACTS AND FIGURES

Belvedere Castle in Vienna was built for the Hapsburg family, who ruled Austria for many centuries.

Longest rivers:
Danube, 2,858 km (1,776 miles);
Rhine, 1,320 km (820 miles).

Largest lakes: Lake Geneva (Switzerland-France), 580 sq km (224 sq miles); Lake Constance (Germany-Switzerland), 539 sq km (208 sq miles).

Largest cities:
Berlin (Germany), 3,300,000;
Hamburg (Germany), 1,576,000;
Vienna (Austria), 1,489,000;
Munich (Germany), 1,269,000;
Cologne (Germany), 927,500;
Zurich (Switzerland), 839,000;
Essen (Germany), 623,000;
Frankfurt (Germany), 618,000.

World's tallest spire:
The cathedral of Ulm in Germany has the world's tallest church spire. It is 161 m (528 ft) high.

Busiest canal: The Kiel Canal in Germany is the busiest in the world. In 1989 over 45,000 ships passed through it on their way between the North Sea and the Baltic Sea.

World's longest road tunnel:
St Gotthard tunnel in Switzerland runs under the Alps, and is 16.32 km (10.14 miles) long.

World's biggest roof: The glass roof over the Olympic Stadium in Munich measures 85,000 sq m (914,940 sq ft).

Many dairy cows graze on the slopes of the Alps. Their milk is used to make the famous Swiss chocolate.

AUSTRIA
Capital: Vienna
Area: 83,853 sq km (32,375 sq miles)
Population: 7,563,000
Language: German
Religion: Christian
Currency: Schilling
Government: Republic

GERMANY
National capital: Berlin
Seat of government: Bonn
Area: 356,910 sq km (137,804 sq miles)
Population: 77,714,000
Language: German
Religion: Christian
Currency: Deutsche Mark
Government: Republic

LIECHTENSTEIN
Capital: Vaduz
Area: 160 sq km (62 sq miles)
Population: 28,000
Language: German
Religion: Christian
Currency: Swiss franc
Government: Monarchy

SWITZERLAND
Capital: Bern
Area: 41,293 sq km (15,943 sq miles)
Population: 6,545,000
Languages: German, French, Italian
Religion: Christian
Currency: Swiss franc
Government: Republic

The city of Munich in southern Germany is famous for its annual beer festival, the Oktoberfest.

GERMANY

C Z E C H O S L O V A K I A

REGENSBURG CATHEDRAL

Regensburg

Beer

Sugar beet

Electronics

Munich
Violins

HOHENSALZBURG CASTLE

Salzburg

MOZART'S BIRTHPLACE

A U S T R I A

Edelweiss

Chamois (type of goat)

Mountain climbing

Skiing

Cakes

Lipizzaner horses

Linz

Danube

VIENNA OPERA HOUSE

VIENNA

Iron and steel

Dairy cattle

Great white heron

MARIA-HILF-KIRCHE (GRAZ)

Graz

H U N G A R Y

AUSTRIA

L   Y   Y U G O S L A V I A

THE RHINE VALLEY

The Rhine is one of the longest rivers in Europe. It flows from Switzerland through Germany and the Netherlands to the North Sea. Boats can sail up the Rhine as far as Basel in Switzerland, and for this reason the river has been an important European trade route for many centuries. Products such as coal, iron ore and petroleum are still transported by barge along the Rhine today.

In western Germany, the Rhine flows through a spectacular, steep-sided valley dotted with ruined castles, some of which are 800 years old. In many places the sides of the valley have been terraced and are used for growing wine grapes.

One of the famous sights of the Rhine Valley is the Lorelei Rock, which is situated west of Wiesbaden. According to legend, a water nymph at the Lorelei sang to passing sailors and lured them to their deaths on the rocks.

A   B   C   D   E   F   G   H   I   J   K   L   M   N   O

13   14   15   16   17   18   19   20   21   22   23

ITALY

THE EASILY RECOGNIZABLE BOOT SHAPE OF ITALY is a thin, 800-km (500-miles) long peninsula in southern Europe, which stretches south into the Mediterranean Sea. Nearly three-quarters of the country is hilly or mountainous. In the north, the snow-covered Alps form a barrier between Italy and the rest of Europe. Running down the spine of the country are the Apennines, rugged mountains dotted with hill-top villages and small towns that have hardly changed for centuries. The Mediterranean islands of Sicily and Sardinia are also part of Italy.

Modern Italy, with Rome as its capital, only came into existence in 1870. Before then the area had been a patchwork of independent city states. These states can still be seen today in Italy's 20 "regions". Two of the states have remained independent – the Vatican City in Rome and the Republic of San Marino in northeastern Italy.

Italy has been important since Roman times, when it was the centre of the greatest empire Europe had ever seen. The remains of Roman roads and buildings can still be seen all over the country and beyond. In the 14th–16th centuries, Italy was the centre of an important movement in the arts, called the Renaissance. Many beautiful paintings, sculptures, buildings, and poems were produced in Italy during this period. Amongst Italy's most famous Renaissance writers and artists were Michelangelo, Leonardo da Vinci, Raphael, and Dante. Today millions of tourists each year visit Italy's ancient cities and art treasures.

Modern Italy is an important industrial nation, with large steel, chemical, textile, and car manufacturing industries. However, many Italians still make their living from farming. The main crops are wheat, corn, rice, grapes, and olives, and there are many fishing ports around Italy's coast.

FACTS AND FIGURES

Cars, motorbikes, tractors and trucks are among Italy's most valuable exports. Major manufactures include Fiat, Ferrari, and Lamborghini.

The city of Venice is built on about 120 islands and has canals in place of streets.

A horse race called the Palio takes place in Siena each year. The riders wear traditional costumes dating from the 15th century.

Highest mountains: Mont Blanc (Italy-France), 4,807 m (15,771 ft); Monte Rosa (Italy-Switzerland), 4,634 m (15,203 ft).

Longest river: Po, 672 km (418 miles).

Largest lakes: Lake Garda, 370 sq km (143 sq miles); Lake Maggiore, 212 sq km (82 sq miles); Lake Como, 145 sq km (55 sq miles).

Largest cities: Rome, 2,816,000; Milan, 1,464,000; Naples, 1,203,000; Turin, 1,012,000.

ITALY
Capital: Rome
Area: 301,268 sq km (116,320 sq miles)
Population: 57,470,000
Language: Italian
Religion: Christian
Currency: Lira
Government: Republic

MALTA
Capital: Valletta
Area: 316 sq km (122 sq miles)
Population: 345,000
Languages: Maltese, English
Religion: Christian
Currency: Maltese pound
Government: Republic

SAN MARINO
Capital: San Marino
Area: 61 sq km (23 sq miles)
Population: 24,000
Language: Italian
Religion: Christian
Currency: Lira
Government: Republic

VATICAN CITY
Area: 0.44 sq km (0.17 sq miles)
Population: 1,000

AUSTRIA

YUGOSLAVIA

SWITZERLAND

FRANCE

ALPS

APENNINES

LIGURIAN SEA

PINNACLES OF THE DOLOMITES

Chamois (type of goat)

Udine

Wine

Trieste

St Mark's Square

Venice

Venetian gondolier

Cruise liner

Tourism

Old Town of San Marino

Sole

Ancona

St Chiara (Assisi)

Assisi

Perugia

Siena

The Palio

Florence Cathedral

Rimini

SAN MARINO

Bolzano

Trento

Padua

Ferrara

Bologna

Ravenna

Po

Florence

Arno

Leaning Tower of Pisa

Pisa

Tourism

Livorno

Squid

ELBA

Verona

Adige

Mantua

Modena

Parma

Ferrari cars

Violins

Cremona

Po

Marble quarry

Tourism

Genoa

La Spezia

Tourism

Tourism

Shellfish

Ferry boat

Marmots

Skiing

LAKE GARDA

Brescia

Bergamo

LAKE COMO

Monza

Milan

Milan Cathedral

Como

LAKE MAGGIORE

Rice

Parmesan cheese

Wine

Tourism

Sardines

MONTE ROSA 4,634 m

MONT BLANC 4,807 m

Ibex (type of goat)

Turin

Fiat cars

Olive trees

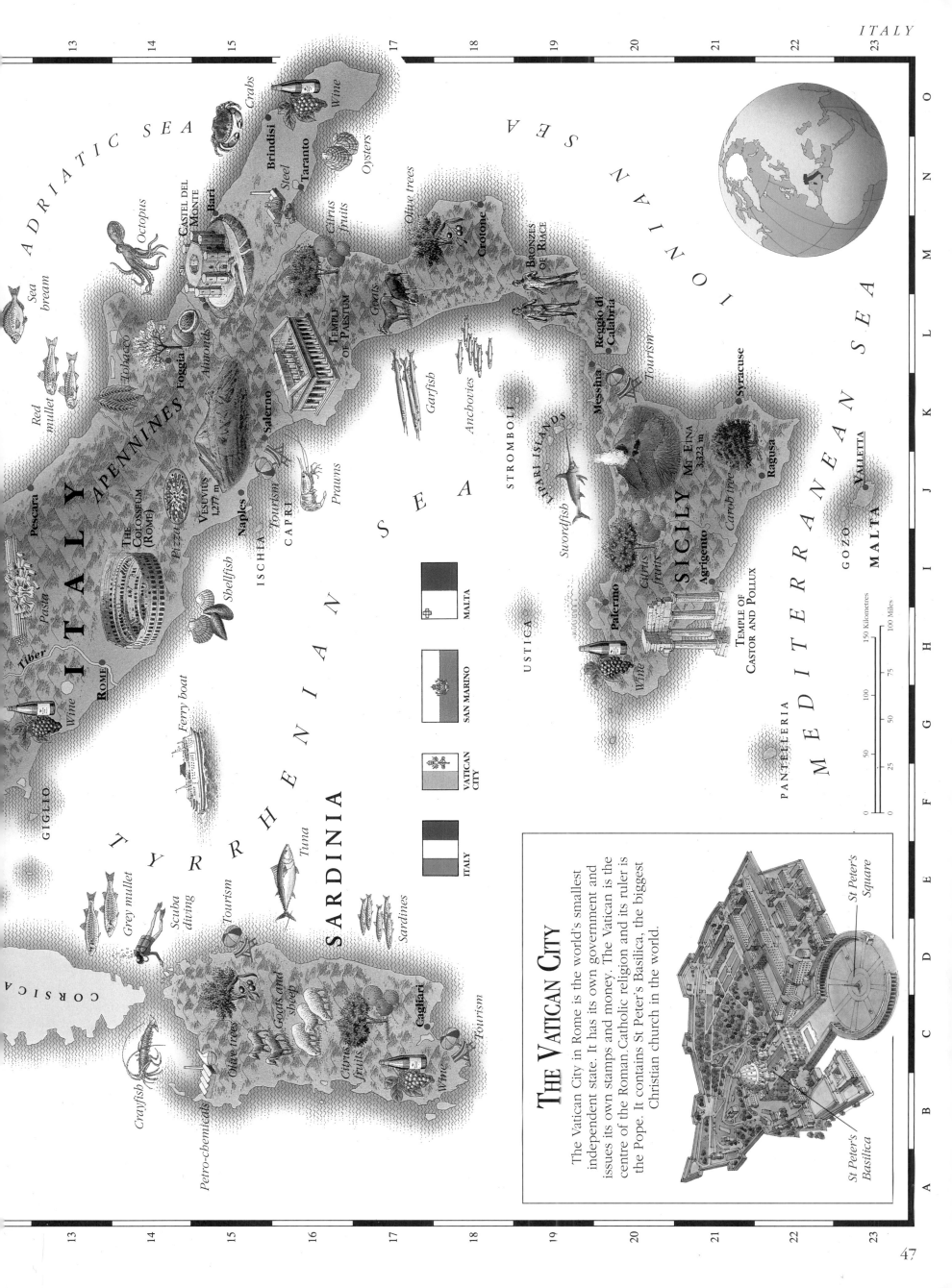

ADRIATIC SEA

IONIAN SEA

TYRRHENIAN SEA

MEDITERRANEAN SEA

ITALY
APENNINES
SARDINIA
SICILY

CORSICA

Crabs
Wine
Brindisi
Steel
Taranto
Oysters
Bari
Citrus fruits
Olive trees
CASTEL DEL MONTE
Octopus
Crotone
Goats
BRONZES OF RIACE
Sea bream
Temple of Paestum
Reggio di Calabria
Red mullet
Foggia
Tobacco
Almonds
Garfish
Anchovies
Messina
Tourism
Syracuse
Pescara
Mt Etna 3,323 m
STROMBOLI
LIPARI ISLANDS
Swordfish
THE COLOSSEUM (ROME)
VESUVIUS 1,277 m
Naples
Salerno
ISCHIA
CAPRI
Tourism
Prawns
USTICA
Palermo
Citrus fruits
Agrigento
Carob tree
Ragusa
Pasta
Wine
ROME
Shellfish
Tiber
Wine
GIGLIO
Ferry boat
Temple of Castor and Pollux
Wine
PANTELLERIA
GOZO
MALTA
VALLETTA

Grey mullet
Scuba diving
Tourism
Tuna
Sardines
Crayfish
Petro-chemicals
Olive trees
Goats and sheep
Citrus fruits
Cagliari
Tourism
Wine

MALTA
SAN MARINO
VATICAN CITY
ITALY

150 Kilometres
100 Miles
100
75
50
50
25
0

THE VATICAN CITY

The Vatican City in Rome is the world's smallest
independent state. It has its own government and
issues its own stamps and money. The Vatican is the
centre of the Roman Catholic religion and its ruler is
the Pope. It contains St Peter's Basilica, the biggest
Christian church in the world.

St Peter's Square

St Peter's Basilica

SPAIN AND PORTUGAL

THE COUNTRIES of Spain and Portugal occupy a large, square block of land called the Iberian Peninsula in the southwest of Europe. The peninsula also contains the tiny independent state of Andorra and the British colony of Gibraltar. Over the centuries, Spain and Portugal have been invaded and settled by many different peoples, including the Romans and the Moors – an Arab people from North Africa who ruled much of Spain for nearly eight centuries.

Both Spain and Portugal have a long history of exploring and trading by sea. Christopher Columbus set out from Spain when he sailed to America in 1492. In 1497 the Portuguese explorer, Vasco da Gama, became the first person to sail around Africa to India. Settlers followed the explorers, and during the 16th century Spain and Portugal came to rule vast empires in North and South America, Asia, and Africa.

Today, many people in Spain and Portugal make their living from farming or fishing. Both countries also have important manufacturing industries, producing steel, ships, cars, chemicals, and textiles. Tourism is a major source of wealth in both countries.

PORTUGAL

THE WINE TRADE

Spain and Portugal are famous for their "fortified" wines, such as sherry and port. These contain more alcohol than normal wine because brandy is added to the grape juice to fortify, or strengthen, it. This was originally done to stop the wine going off while it was shipped abroad. Fortified wines are left in wooden casks to mature for at least three years. Both sherry and port are named after the towns where they are produced – sherry comes from Jerez de la Frontera in southern Spain, and port from Porto in northern Portugal.

BAY OF BISCA

ATLANTIC OCEAN

Shellfish
Fish packing
Iron and steel
Horses
La Coruña
Gijón
Apples
Santander
Oviedo
Coal
CAVE PAINTING (ALTAMIRA)
CATHEDRAL OF SANTIAGO DE COMPOSTELA
Santiago
Brown bear
León
Fish packing
Vigo
Minho
Potatoes
LEÓN CATHEDRAL
Cattle
Wheat
COCKEREL OF BARCELOS
Egyptian vulture
Textiles
Braga
Valladolid
Anchovies
Porto
Cattle
S   P
Douro
Port wine
Salamanca
HOUSE OF SHELLS (SALAMANCA)
Segovia
Mackerel
Transporting port wine
Potatoes
Fish packing
Avila
Rugs
Coimbra
STATUE OF PIZARRO (TRUJILLO)
Pilchards
PORTUGAL
Tagus
Toledo
TOLEDO CATHEDRAL
BELEM TOWER
Olive trees
Wine
ROMAN THEATRE
Tagus
ROMAN TEMPLE (EVORA)
Merida
Guadiana
Manchego cheese
LISBON
Sheep
Badajoz
Windmill
Setúbal
Bulls
CÓRDOBA MOSQUE
Fish packing
Sardines
SEVILLE CATHEDRAL
Córdoba
Guadalquivir
Cork oak
Citrus fruits
Holy week procession (Seville)
Tourism
Guadiana
Pardel lynx
Seville
Tourism
Faro
Málaga
Wine
Lobster
Sherry
Jerez de la Frontera
ROCK OF GIBRALTAR
Cádiz
GIBRALTAR
STRAIT OF GIBRALTAR
ME
Ceuta (Spain)
Tuna

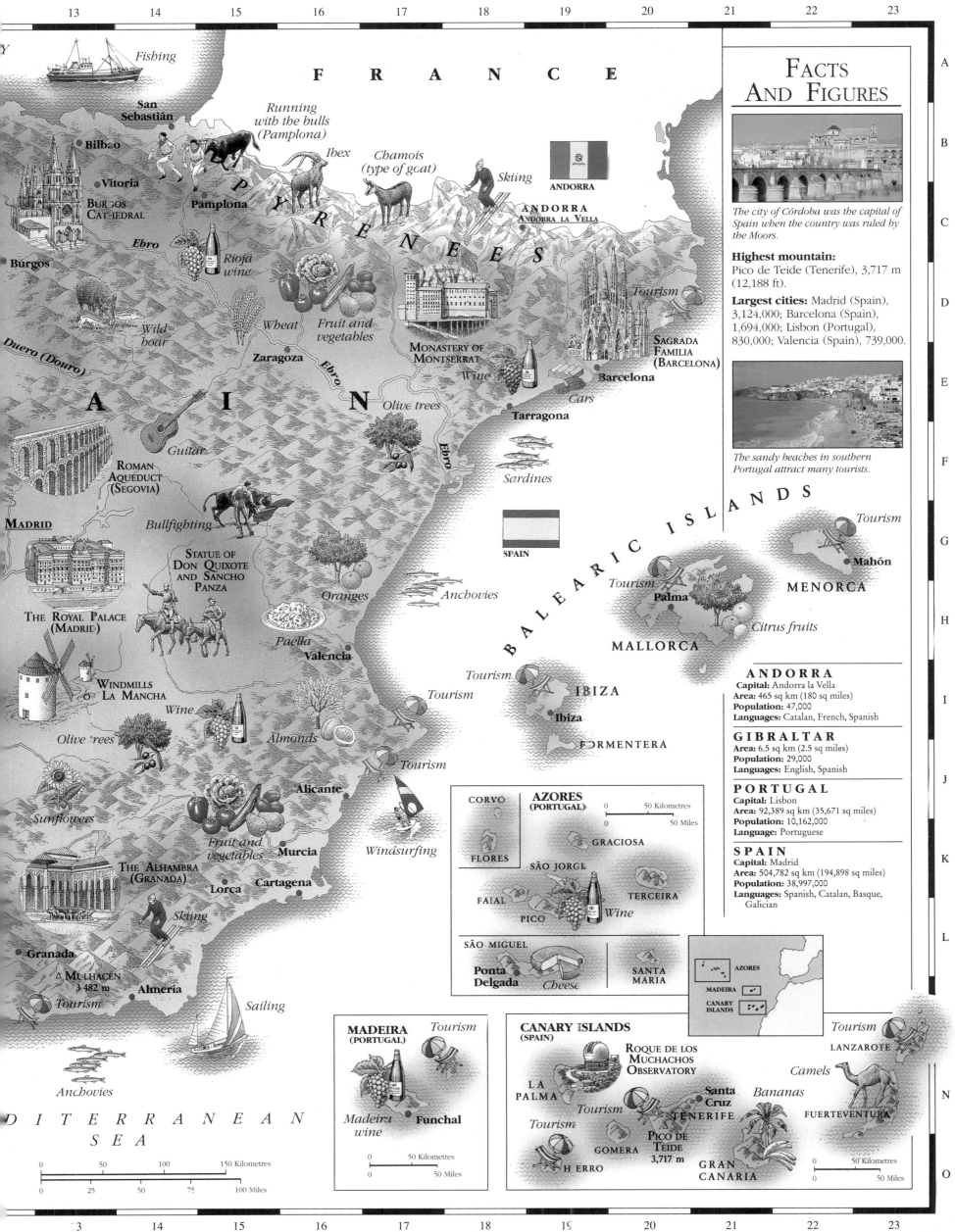

13 14 15 16 17 18 19 20 21 22 23

Fishing

F R A N C E

San
Sebastián

Bilbao

**Running
with the bulls
(Pamplona)**

Ibex

*Chamois
(type of goat)*

Skiing

ANDORRA

Vitoria

BURGOS
CATHEDRAL

Pamplona

ANDORRA
Andorra la Vella

Burgos

Ebro

P Y R E N E E S

*Rioja
wine*

Tourism

Duero (Douro)

*Wild
boar*

Zaragoza

Wheat

*Fruit and
vegetables*

**MONASTERY OF
MONTSERRAT**

Ebro

**SAGRADA
FAMÍLIA
(BARCELONA)**

A I N

Wine

Barcelona

Olive trees

Cars

Tarragona

Ebro

ROMAN
AQUEDUCT
(SEGOVIA)

Guitar

MADRID

Sardines

B A L E A R I C   I S L A N D S

Tourism

SPAIN

THE ROYAL PALACE
(MADRID)

Bullfighting

STATUE OF
DON QUIXOTE
AND SANCHO
PANZA

Oranges

Anchovies

Tourism

Mahón

MENORCA

Tourism

Palma

Citrus fruits

MALLORCA

Paella

WINDMILLS
OF LA MANCHA

Valencia

Tourism

IBIZA

Tourism

Wine

Ibiza

Olive trees

Almonds

FORMENTERA

FACTS
AND FIGURES

The city of Córdoba was the capital of
Spain when the country was ruled by
the Moors.

Highest mountain:
Pico de Teide (Tenerife), 3,717 m
(12,188 ft).

Largest cities: Madrid (Spain),
3,124,000; Barcelona (Spain),
1,694,000; Lisbon (Portugal),
830,000; Valencia (Spain), 739,000.

The sandy beaches in southern
Portugal attract many tourists.

ANDORRA
Capital: Andorra la Vella
Area: 465 sq km (180 sq miles)
Population: 47,000
Languages: Catalan, French, Spanish

GIBRALTAR
Area: 6.5 sq km (2.5 sq miles)
Population: 29,000
Languages: English, Spanish

PORTUGAL
Capital: Lisbon
Area: 92,389 sq km (35,671 sq miles)
Population: 10,162,000
Language: Portuguese

SPAIN
Capital: Madrid
Area: 504,782 sq km (194,898 sq miles)
Population: 38,997,000
Languages: Spanish, Catalan, Basque,
Galician

Sunflowers

Tourism

Wine

Tourism

Windsurfing

Alicante

*Fruit and
vegetables*

Murcia

THE ALHAMBRA
(GRANADA)

Skiing

Lorca

Cartagena

**AZORES
(PORTUGAL)**

CORVO

0 ____ 50 Kilometres

0 ____ 50 Miles

FLORES

GRACIOSA

SÃO JORGE

FAIAL

PICO

TERCEIRA

Wine

Granada

△ MULHACÉN
3 482 m

Almería

Tourism

Sailing

SÃO MIGUEL

Ponta
Delgada

Cheese

SANTA
MARIA

AZORES

MADEIRA

CANARY
ISLANDS

Anchovies

M E D I T E R R A N E A N

S E A

**MADEIRA
(PORTUGAL)**

Tourism

*Madeira
wine*

Funchal

**CANARY ISLANDS
(SPAIN)**

ROQUE DE LOS
MUCHACHOS
OBSERVATORY

LA
PALMA

Tourism

Santa
Cruz

TENERIFE

Bananas

Tourism

LANZAROTE

Camels

FUERTEVENTURA

Tourism

GOMERA

PICO DE
TEIDE
3,717 m

GRAN
CANARIA

0 ____ 50 Kilometres

0 ____ 50 Miles

HIERRO

0 50 100 150 Kilometres

0 25 50 75 100 Miles

0 ____ 50 Kilometres

0 ____ 50 Miles

CENTRAL AND EASTERN EUROPE

THIS REGION has always been one of the most unstable parts of Europe, and the boundaries between the countries have changed many times. After World War II, all the countries in this region, apart from Greece, became part of the "Eastern Bloc". They had communist governments and strong links with the USSR. In recent years there have been important political changes in the region. Many of the countries are now establishing democratic forms of government and are building closer links with their neighbours in Western Europe.

The northern part of this region is dominated by Poland. The country of Poland has been much fought over, and for long periods it did not exist as a separate nation. Poland is rich in coal and copper, and has large textile, iron, steel, and shipbuilding industries. Farming is also important: the main crops are potatoes, wheat, and sugar beet. Czechoslovakia was only created as an independent country in 1918. The country is made up of two separate peoples, the Czechs and the Slovaks, each speaking a different language. Many Czechoslovaks are farmers, but the country also has important coal, iron, and steel industries.

To the south lies the area known as the Balkans, which includes the countries of Greece, Albania, Yugoslavia, Bulgaria, Romania and Hungary. The present pattern of countries in the Balkans was only formed during the rearrangement of European borders at the end of the two World Wars. Yugoslavia has a large tourist industry with popular beaches along its Adriatic coast. Greece, too, is one of the most popular holiday destinations in Europe and visitors go there to explore its many islands and ancient buildings.

FACTS AND FIGURES

Every year many tourists visit the picturesque old towns along Yugoslavia's Adriatic coast.

Largest cities: Budapest (Hungary), 3,962,000; Athens (Greece), 3,020,000.

Longest river: Danube, 2,858 km (1,776 miles).

Highest mountains: Musala (Bulgaria), 2,925 m (9,596 ft); Mt Olympus (Greece), 2,917 m (9,570 ft).

Warsaw, in Poland, was badly damaged during World War II, but many old buildings have been rebuilt.

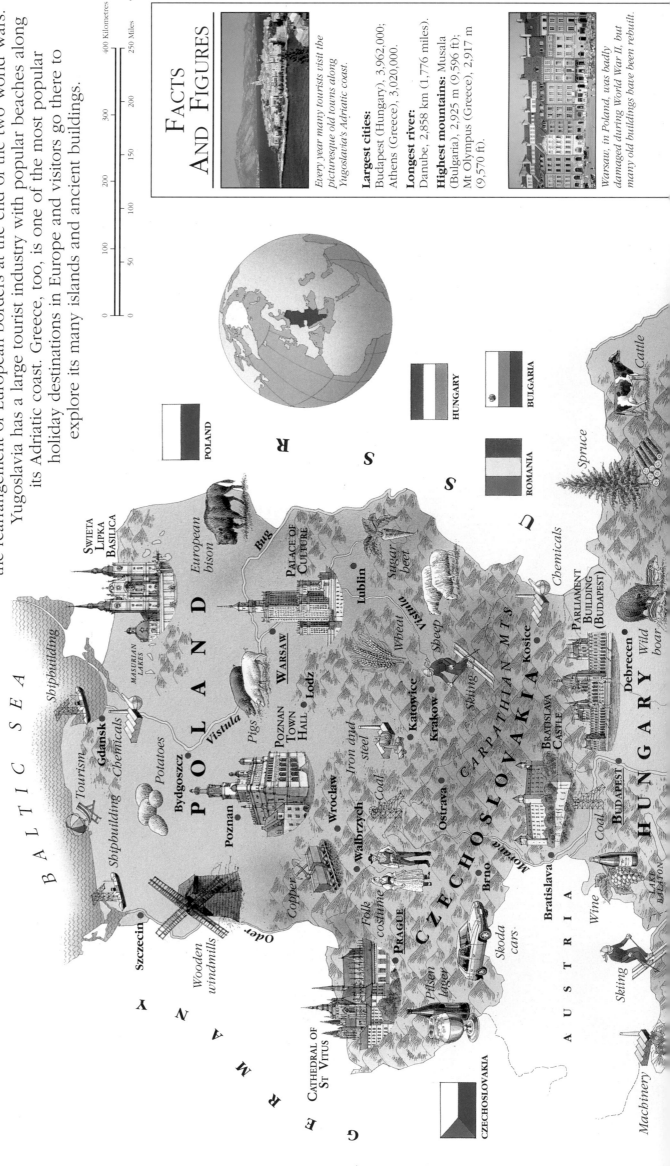

400 Kilometres
250 Miles
300
200
150
200
100
100
50
0
0

POLAND

HUNGARY

BULGARIA

ROMANIA

CZECHOSLOVAKIA

BALTIC SEA

Shipbuilding

Tourism

Gdansk Chemicals

Shipbuilding

Potatoes

Bydgoszcz

Szczecin

Wooden windmills

Copper

Poznan

POZNAN TOWN HALL

Vistula

Pigs

MASURIAN LAKES

European bison

SWIETA LIPKA BASILICA

Bug

PALACE OF CULTURE

WARSAW

Lodz

Lublin

Sugar beet

Wheat

Vistula

Sheep

P O L A N D

Iron and steel

Coal

Wroclaw

Walbrzych

Katowice

Krakow

Skiing

CARPATHIAN MTS

Kosice

Folk costume

PRAGUE

Pilsen lager

CATHEDRAL OF ST VITUS

Skoda cars

Brno

Morava

Ostrava

C Z E C H O S L O V A K I A

Bratislava

BRATISLAVA CASTLE

Wine

Coal

BUDAPEST

H U N G A R Y

PARLIAMENT BUILDING (BUDAPEST)

Debrecen Wild boar

Skiing

LAKE BALATON

A U S T R I A

G E R M A N Y

Oder

Chemicals

Spruce

Cattle

Machinery

R U S S I A

ALBANIA
Capital: Tirana
Area: 28,748 sq km (11,099 sq miles)
Population: 3,145,000
Language: Albanian
Religions: Moslem, Christian
Currency: Lek
Government: Communist republic

BULGARIA
Capital: Sofia
Area: 110,912 sq km (42,823 sq miles)
Population: 8,995,000
Language: Bulgarian
Religions: Christian, Moslem
Currency: Lev
Government: Republic

CZECHOSLOVAKIA
Capital: Prague
Area: 127,876 sq km (49,373 sq miles)
Population: 15,610,000
Languages: Czech, Slovak
Religions: Christian
Currency: Koruna
Government: Republic

GREECE
Capital: Athens
Area: 131,990 sq km (50,961 sq miles)
Population: 10,030,000
Language: Greek
Religion: Christian
Currency: Drachma
Government: Republic

HUNGARY
Capital: Budapest
Area: 93,032 sq km (35,919 sq miles)
Population: 10,604,000
Language: Hungarian
Religion: Christian
Currency: Forint
Government: Republic

POLAND
Capital: Warsaw
Area: 312,685 sq km (120,728 sq miles)
Population: 37,873,000
Language: Polish
Religion: Christian
Currency: Zloty
Government: Republic

ROMANIA
Capital: Bucharest
Area: 237,500 sq km (91,699 sq miles)
Population: 23,052,000
Languages: Romanian
Religion: Christian
Currency: Leu
Government: Republic

YUGOSLAVIA
Capital: Belgrade
Area: 255,804 sq km (98,766 sq miles)
Population: 23,552,000
Languages: Serbo-Croat, Albanian, Macedonian, Slovene
Religion: Christian
Currency: Dinar
Government: Republic

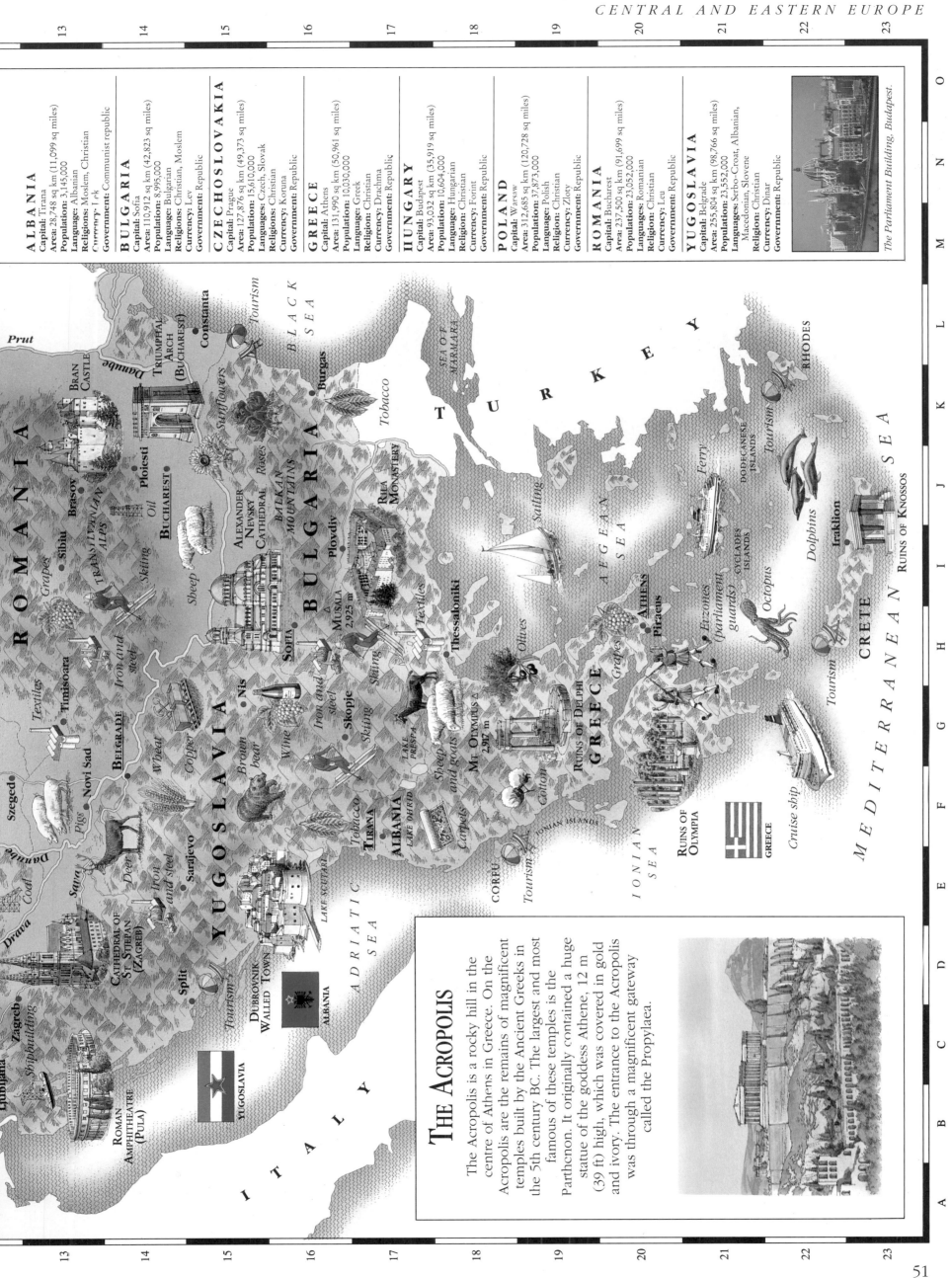

The Parliament Building, Budapest.

THE ACROPOLIS

The Acropolis is a rocky hill in the centre of Athens in Greece. On the Acropolis are the remains of magnificent temples built by the Ancient Greeks in the 5th century BC. The largest and most famous of these temples is the Parthenon. It originally contained a huge statue of the goddess Athene, 12 m (39 ft) high, which was covered in gold and ivory. The entrance to the Acropolis was through a magnificent gateway called the Propylaea.

51

ASIA

Guilin, China.

ASIA is the largest continent in the world, occupying nearly a third of the world's total land area. It contains the world's highest point (Mount Everest), as well as its lowest (the Dead Sea). Asia also has the largest population of any continent – six out of every ten people in the world live there. All the world's major religions – including Judaism, Islam, Buddhism, Christianity, Confucianism, and Hinduism – originated in Asia.

In a continent of this size, stretching from the Arctic to the Equator, there are great contrasts. The climate ranges from some of the coldest places on Earth to some of the hottest, and from some of the driest places to some of the wettest. Asia contains the world's largest country (the USSR) and some of its smallest countries. In parts of Asia there are huge concentrations of people, yet there are also vast regions which are almost uninhabited.

Siberia, the Asian part of the USSR, is mainly covered by coniferous forest. It is bitterly cold in winter, and few people live there. Bordering the USSR in the east is China. Most of China's one billion people live in the eastern part of the country where the land is good for farming.

The population of the Gobi Desert and the high plateau of Tibet is very small. South of the Himalayas, the world's highest mountain range, lies Southern Asia, which is often called the Indian subcontinent. Around one billion people live there, mainly along the fertile coasts and on the plains of the Ganges and Indus rivers in the north.

Southwestern Asia is also known as the Middle East. The world's earliest-known civilizations grew up here in the area called the Fertile Crescent, which extends from the Mediterranean Sea across Syria to the land between the Tigris and Euphrates rivers. Among the ancient peoples of the Fertile Crescent were the Sumerians, Assyrians, Babylonians, and Hebrews. This area contrasts sharply with the almost empty deserts of the Arabian Peninsula, flanked by the oil-rich nations of the Persian Gulf, such as Saudi Arabia, Qatar, and Bahrain.

Southeastern Asia is situated along the Equator. Much of the region is made up of thousands of islands, large and small. These include the countries of Indonesia, Malaysia, and the Philippines.

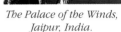
The Palace of the Winds, Jaipur, India.

Bronze Buddah, Kamakura, Japan.

FACTS ABOUT ASIA

Area: 43,608,000 sq km (16,838,365 sq miles).

Population: 3,074,000,000.

Number of independent countries: 42 (this includes 6 per cent of Egypt, 97 per cent of Turkey, and 75 per cent of the USSR).

Largest countries: The Asian part of the USSR, 16,831,000 sq km (6,498,500 sq miles) – this is only 75 per cent of the total area of the USSR; China, 9,597,000 sq km (3,705,691 sq miles).

Most populated countries: China, 1,083,889,000 (the largest population in the world); India, 813,990,000.

Largest cities: Shanghai (China), 12,320,000; Tokyo (Japan), 8,209,000; Seoul (South Korea), 6,889,470.

Highest mountains: Mt Everest (Nepal-China), the highest in the world, 8,848 m (29,028 ft); K2 (Mt Godwin Austen) (Pakistan-China), 8,611 m (28,250 ft).

Longest rivers: Chang Jiang (Yangtze), 6,300 km (3,915 miles); Huang He (Yellow River), 5,463 km (3,395 miles); Ob-Irtysh, 5,410 km (3,362 miles); Amur, 4,443 km (2,761 miles).

Main deserts: Gobi (Mongolia-China), about 1,295,000 sq km (500,000 sq miles); Thar (Pakistan-India), about 192,000 sq km (74,000 sq miles).

Largest lakes: Caspian Sea (USSR-Iran), the largest in the world, 371,000 sq km (143,205 sq miles); Aral Sea (USSR), 65,500 sq km (25,285 sq miles).

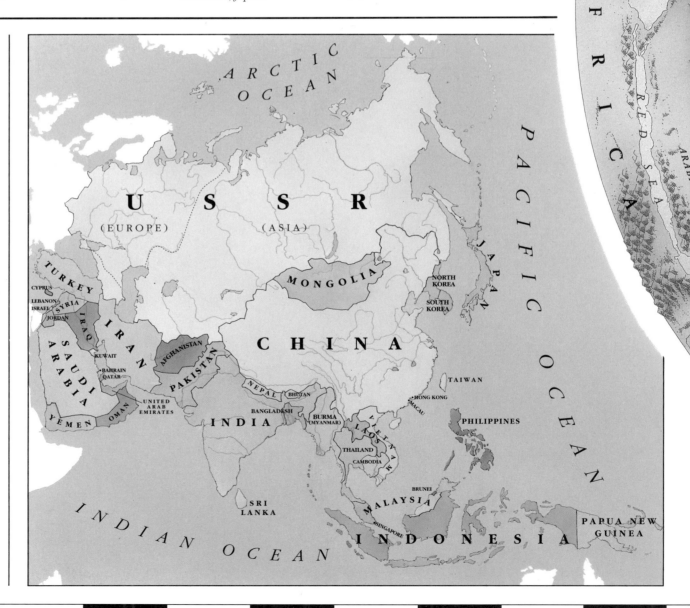

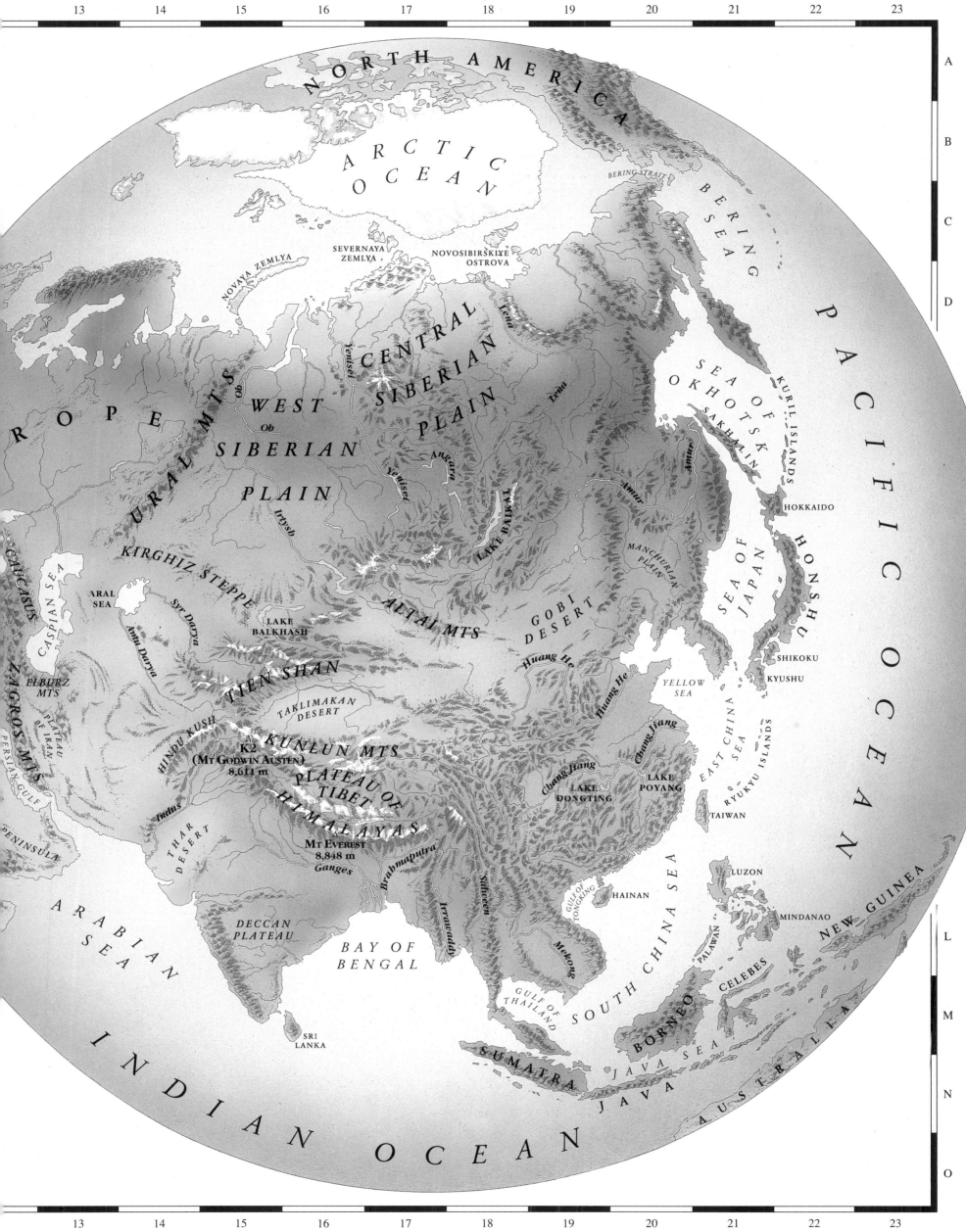

13 14 15 16 17 18 19 20 21 22 23

A

B

C

D

NORTH AMERICA

ARCTIC OCEAN

BERING STRAIT

BERING SEA

PACIFIC OCEAN

NOVAYA ZEMLYA

SEVERNAYA ZEMLYA

NOVOSIBIRSKIYE OSTROVA

KURIL ISLANDS

SEA OF OKHOTSK

SAKHALIN

HOKKAIDO

Lena

CENTRAL SIBERIAN PLAIN

Yenisei

Ob

WEST SIBERIAN PLAIN

URAL MTS

Ob

Irtysh

Yenisei

Angara

Lena

LAKE BAIKAL

Amur

Amur

MANCHURIAN PLAIN

SEA OF JAPAN

HONSHU

ROPE

CAUCASUS

CASPIAN SEA

ARAL SEA

Syr Darya

KIRGHIZ STEPPE

LAKE BALKHASH

Amu Darya

ALTAI MTS

GOBI DESERT

Huang He

SHIKOKU

KYUSHU

YELLOW SEA

ELBURZ MTS

ZAGROS MTS

PLATEAU OF IRAN

PERSIAN GULF

TIEN SHAN

TAKLIMAKAN DESERT

HINDU KUSH

K2 (MT GODWIN AUSTEN) 8,611 m

KUNLUN MTS

PLATEAU OF TIBET

Huang He

Chang Jiang

Chang Jiang

LAKE DONGTING

LAKE POYANG

EAST CHINA SEA

RYUKYU ISLANDS

TAIWAN

Indus

THAR DESERT

HIMALAYAS

MT EVEREST 8,848 m

Ganges

Brahmaputra

Salween

Irrawaddy

GULF OF TONGKING

HAINAN

LUZON

MINDANAO

NEW GUINEA

ARABIAN SEA

DECCAN PLATEAU

BAY OF BENGAL

Mekong

SOUTH CHINA SEA

PALAWAN

CELEBES

BORNEO

GULF OF THAILAND

L

M

SRI LANKA

SUMATRA

JAVA

JAVA SEA

AUSTRALIA

N

O

INDIAN OCEAN

13 14 15 16 17 18 19 20 21 22 23

USSR

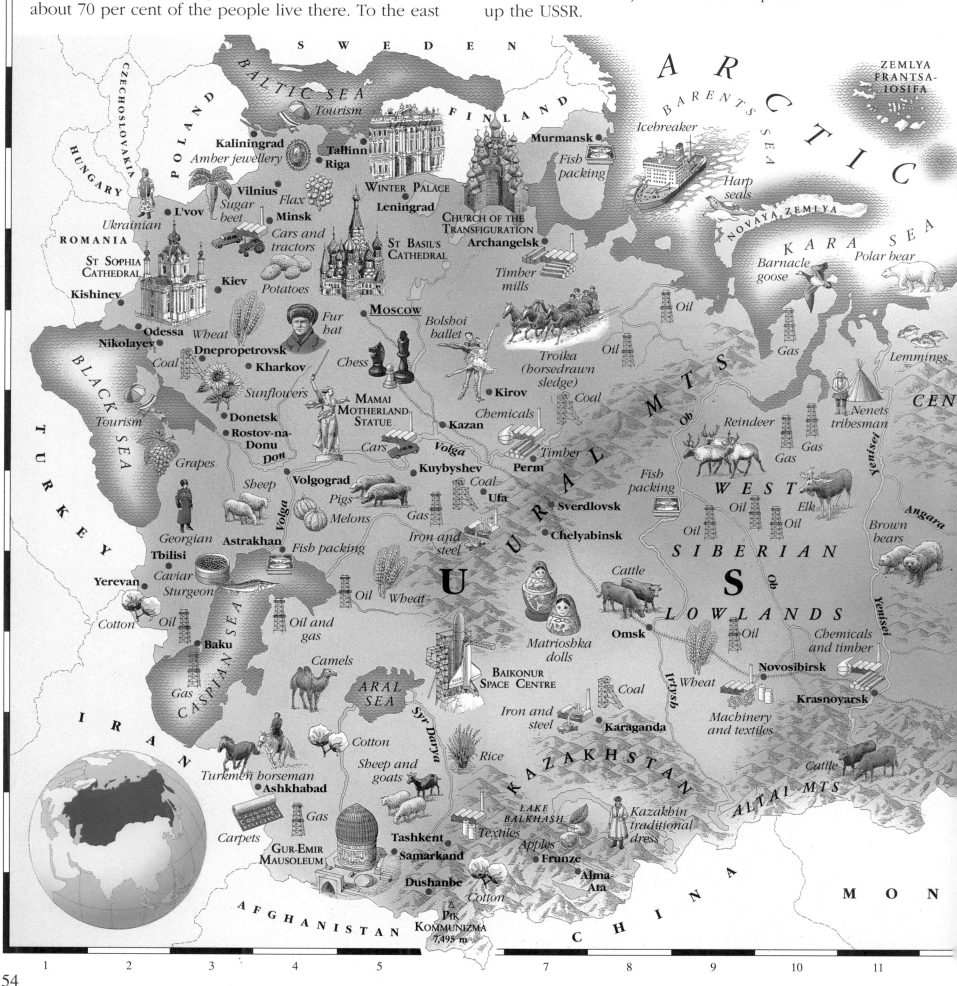

THE UNION OF SOVIET SOCIALIST REPUBLICS, or USSR, is the largest country in the world. It is more than twice the size of Canada, the second largest. It stretches about 9,700 km (6,000 miles) from east to west and includes more than one-seventh of the world's total land area.

The USSR spreads across two continents – Europe and Asia. The Ural mountains divide them, with Europe to the west and Asia to the east. The European part of the USSR occupies only 25 per cent of the land area, but about 70 per cent of the people live there. To the east

lies Siberia. Much of this region is a huge, uninhabited wilderness with vast pine forests, but it is rich in precious stones and oil. In winter, the temperature in northern Siberia regularly falls below -45°C (-49°F).

The USSR is made up of 15 republics and many more smaller regions. Many different peoples – such as the Georgians, the Uzbeks, and the Russians – live in the USSR. Sometimes the country is called Russia, but this is incorrect: Russia is just one of the republics which make up the USSR.

Map labels:

CZECHOSLOVAKIA · HUNGARY · ROMANIA · POLAND · SWEDEN · FINLAND · TURKEY · IRAN · AFGHANISTAN · CHINA · MON · CEN

ARCTIC · BALTIC SEA · BARENTS SEA · KARA SEA · BLACK SEA · CASPIAN SEA · ARAL SEA · NOVAYA ZEMLYA · ZEMLYA FRANTSA-IOSIFA

URAL MTS · WEST SIBERIAN LOWLANDS · KAZAKHSTAN · ALTAI MTS · USSR

Ob · Yenisei · Angara · Irtysh · Syr Darya · Don · Volga

Kaliningrad · Tallinn · Riga · Vilnius · L'vov · Minsk · Leningrad · Murmansk · Archangelsk · Kishinev · Kiev · Odessa · Nikolayev · Dnepropetrovsk · Kharkov · Moscow · Kirov · Kazan · Perm · Donetsk · Rostov-na-Donu · Kuybyshev · Ufa · Sverdlovsk · Chelyabinsk · Volgograd · Astrakhan · Tbilisi · Yerevan · Baku · Omsk · Novosibirsk · Krasnoyarsk · Karaganda · Ashkhabad · Tashkent · Samarkand · Dushanbe · Frunze · Alma-Ata

Tourism · Amber jewellery · Sugar beet · Flax · Ukrainian · St Sophia Cathedral · Cars and tractors · Potatoes · St Basil's Cathedral · Winter Palace · Church of the Transfiguration · Icebreaker · Fish packing · Harp seals · Polar bear · Barnacle goose · Timber mills · Oil · Gas · Lemmings · Fur hat · Chess · Bolshoi ballet · Troika (horsedrawn sledge) · Coal · Chemicals · Mamai Motherland Statue · Cars · Reindeer · Nenets tribesman · Sunflowers · Wheat · Coal · Timber · Fish packing · Elk · Brown bears · Sheep · Pigs · Melons · Gas · Iron and steel · Cattle · Oil · Grapes · Georgian · Fish packing · Caviar · Sturgeon · Oil · Wheat · Matrioshka dolls · Cotton · Oil · Oil and gas · Camels · Baikonur Space Centre · Coal · Machinery and textiles · Turkmen horseman · Cotton · Sheep and goats · Rice · Iron and steel · Kazakhin traditional dress · Cattle · Gas · Carpets · Gur-Emir Mausoleum · Textiles · Apples · Cotton · Pik Kommunizma 7,495 m

THE KREMLIN

The Kremlin fortress is the oldest part of Moscow. The present walls date from the late 1400s and inside are cathedrals and palaces. The Great Kremlin Palace was once the home of the tsars (emperors), but now the Supreme Soviet, the government of the USSR, meets there. Outside the Kremlin is Red Square, where a May Day parade is held each year to celebrate the Russian Revolution of 1917. On Red Square is the Lenin Mausoleum, containing the preserved body of Lenin, the "Father of the Revolution".

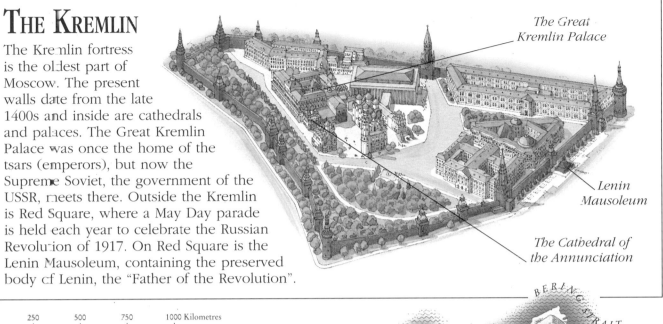

The Great Kremlin Palace

Lenin Mausoleum

The Cathedral of the Annunciation

FACTS AND FIGURES

The Cathedral of the Annunciation, the Kremlin, Moscow.

Highest mountain: Pik Kommunizma (Communism Peak), 7,495 m (24,590 ft).

Largest lake: Caspian Sea (the largest lake in the world) covers an area of 371,000 sq km (143,205 sq miles).

World's longest canal system: V I Lenin Volga-Baltic Waterway, 2,430 km (1,510 miles) long.

World's longest railway: Trans-Siberian, Moscow to Nakhoda near Vladivostok, 9,438 km (5,864 miles).

Leningrad, which was once called St Petersburg, was the country's capital city from 1712 until 1918.

USSR
Capital: Moscow
Population: 285,659,000
Area: 22,402,200 sq km (8,649,498 sq miles)
Languages: Russian, many regional languages
Religions: Christian, Moslem, Jewish

UNION REPUBLICS:

ARMENIA
Capital: Yerevan

AZERBAIJAN
Capital: Baku

BYELORUSSIA
Capital: Minsk

ESTONIA
Capital: Tallinn

GEORGIA
Capital: Tbilisi

KAZAKHSTAN
Capital: Alma-Ata

KIRGHIZIA
Capital: Frunze

LATVIA
Capital: Riga

LITHUANIA
Capital: Vilnius

MOLDAVIA
Capital: Kishinev

RUSSIAN SOVIET FEDERAL SOCIALIST REPUBLIC (RSFSR)
Capital: Moscow

TAJIKISTAN
Capital: Dushanbe

TURKMENISTAN
Capital: Ashkhabad

UKRAINE
Capital: Kiev

UZBEKISTAN
Capital: Tashkent

1   2   3   4   5   6   7   8   9   10   11

SOUTHWESTERN ASIA

SOUTHWEST ASIA, also known as the Middle East, lies between three continents – Asia, Africa, and Europe. It contains many varied landscapes and cultures. The countries surrounding the Mediterranean are wetter than the others, and crops such as citrus fruits, olives, and wheat are grown here. To the south stretch the huge deserts of Saudi Arabia. Earlier this century, the world's largest deposits of oil were discovered in the countries around the Persian Gulf. The oil-fields in the region now supply the world.

Some of the world's first settled farming communities and towns, such as Jericho in Jordan, grew up in the rich farmlands of the Fertile Crescent, which stretches from the Mediterranean to the area between the Tigris and Euphrates rivers. In recent years, Southwest Asia has been an unsettled region, troubled by a revolution in Iran and a long and bitter war between Iran and Iraq. Civil war in Lebanon has claimed many lives, and there have also been wars between Israel and its Arab neighbours.

CYPRUS

SYRIA

LEBANON

ISRAEL

JORDAN

SAUDI ARABIA

Mosque of Suleiman I
Istanbul
Bursa
Cherries
Nargle pipe
BLACK SEA
Tobacco
Tourism
PONTINE MTS
Ibis
Cotton
ANKARA
Shish kebab
Tourism
RUINS OF EPHESUS
Carpets
TURKEY
Sheep
Goats
HEAD OF HERCULES
Izmir
Konya
SELEMIYE MOSQUE
Tourism
Whirling dervish
Adana
BODRUM CASTLE
Harran domed dwellings
Oil
Aleppo
Euphrates
Sailing
Grapes
Cotton
NICOSIA
Cedar
SYRIA
CYPRUS
BEIRUT
DAMASCUS
Goats
IR
Haifa
Silk
Tel Aviv-Yafo
AMMAN
Sheep
JERUSALEM
Oranges
JORDAN
SINAI
Bedouin tent
Aqaba
Camels
PETRA (THE KHAZNEH)
AN
GULF OF SUEZ
AL HIJAZ
NAFUD
SAUDI
Coral
Traditional dress
Dates
Pearls
Medina
Yanbu
Petrochemicals
RED
THE GREAT MOSQUE
Jiddah
Mecca
Roses
Sharks
Baboons
SEA
Wheat
Barracuda
Coffee

JERUSALEM

Dome of the Rock

Wailing Wall

Jerusalem is a holy place for Christians, Moslems, and Jews, and it is visited by millions of people each year. The Church of the Holy Sepulchre is built where Christians believe Christ was buried. The gold-topped Dome of the Rock is a mosque built where Moslems believe Mohammed ascended into heaven. The Wailing Wall, where Jews go to pray, is all that remains of the Jewish Temple built by King Herod in the 1st century BC.

1   2   3   4   5   6   7   8   9   10   11

FACTS AND FIGURES

Dhow (Arab boat) off the Yemen coast.

Largest city: Tehran (Iran), 6,043,000.

Hottest capital: Riyadh, in Saudi Arabia, is the hottest capital city in the world, with average July temperatures of over 40°C (104°F).

Sand dunes in the Rub al Khali (The Empty Quarter) in Saudi Arabia. Dunes are formed by the wind, which blows the sand into mounds.

BAHRAIN
Capital: Al Manamah
Area: 678 sq km (262 sq miles)

CYPRUS
Capital: Nicosia
Area: 9,251 sq km (3,571 sq miles)

IRAN
Capital: Tehran
Area: 1,648,000 sq km (636,297 sq miles)

IRAQ
Capital: Baghdad
Area: 438,317 sq km (169,235 sq miles)

ISRAEL
Capital: Jerusalem
Area: 20,770 sq km (8,017 sq miles)

JORDAN
Capital: Amman
Area: 97,740 sq km (37,737 sq miles)

KUWAIT
Capital: Kuwait
Area: 17,818 sq km (6,879 sq miles)

LEBANON
Capital: Beirut
Area: 10,400 sq km (4,015 sq miles)

OMAN
Capital: Muscat
Area: 212,457 sq km (82,030 sq miles)

QATAR
Capital: Doha
Area: 11,000 sq km (4,247 sq miles)

SAUDI ARABIA
Capital: Riyadh
Area: 2,149,690 sq km (830,001 sq miles)*

SYRIA
Capital: Damascus
Area: 185,180 sq km (71,500 sq miles)

TURKEY
Capital: Ankara
Area: 779,452 sq km (300,948 sq miles)

UNITED ARAB EMIRATES
Capital: Abu Dhabi
Area: 83,600 sq km (32,278 sq miles)

YEMEN
Capital: San'a'
Area: 527,968 sq km (203,850 sq miles)

SOUTHERN ASIA

THE LARGEST COUNTRY in Southern Asia is India, and the region is often called the "Indian subcontinent". Over one billion people live in Southern Asia – around 22 per cent of the world's total population.

Most people in Southern Asia live in the wetter areas on the coasts and on the fertile plains of the Indus and Ganges rivers. Nearly three-quarters of the people earn their living from farming. Water is vital, and farmers depend on the monsoon rains, which fall between May and November. The most important crop is rice.

India was united in the 16th and 17th centuries under the Mogul emperors. Then, in the 18th century, the country became part of the British Empire. India gained independence from Britain in 1947, when it was divided into two countries with different religions: Moslem Pakistan and Hindu India. In 1971 the eastern part of Pakistan became a separate country, called Bangladesh.

Today Pakistan and India are the most industrial countries in Southern Asia. Pakistan has textile, food processing, and chemical industries. India produces oil, coal, iron ore, manganese, and copper, and has a variety of industries, including iron and steel, car manufacturing, and computers.

THE TAJ MAHAL

The Taj Mahal was built near Agra in northern India by the Mogul Emperor, Shah Jehan, as a burial place for his wife, the Empress Mumtaz Mahal. It was built between 1630 and 1650 and about 20,000 labourers worked on the building. The Taj Mahal is made of white marble, which was brought 500 km (310 miles) from Rajasthan. The interior is decorated with precious and semi-precious stones.

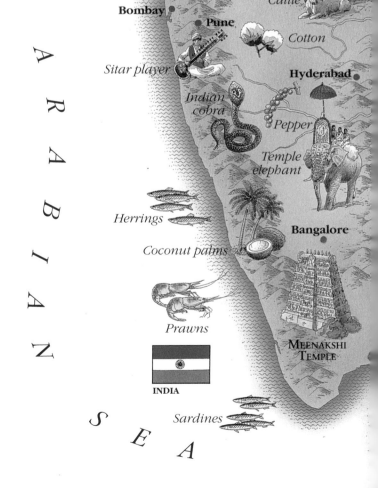

MOUNTAIN PEAKS IN THE HIMALAYAS

MT EVEREST
8,848 m

KANCHENJUNGA
8,586 m

MAKALU I
8,481 m

DHAULAGIRI
8,172 m

NANGA PARBAT
8,126 m

FACTS AND FIGURES

Fishermen at Negombo, Sri Lanka.

Largest cities:
Calcutta (India), 9,194,000;
Bombay (India), 8,243,000;
Delhi (India), 5,729,000;
Karachi (Pakistan), 5,180,000;
Madras (India), 4,277,000;
Dhaka (Bangladesh), 3,440,000.

Longest river:
Indus, 2,896 km (1,800 miles).

Largest island: Sri Lanka,
65,610 sq km (25,325 sq miles).

Highest mountains:
Everest (Nepal-China), 8,848 m
(29,028 ft); K2 (Mt Godwin
Austen) (Pakistan-China), 8,611 m
(28,250 ft); Kanchenjunga (India-
Nepal), 8,586 m (28,170 ft).

**World's heaviest recorded
annual rainfall:** Cherrapunji, in
northeast India, received 26.4 m
(1,042 in) of rain between
August 1860 and July 1861.

*Many Nepalese farmers keep yaks,
which are used as pack animals. They
also provide milk, meat, and wool.*

CHINA

Yaks

MT EVEREST
8,848 m

Red
panda

N E P A L

KATHMANDU

H I M A L A Y A S

Picking
tea

THIMPHU

BHUTAN

Sugar-cane

Rice

Ganges

Indian rhinoceros

Cycle
rickshaw

Rubies

Jade

Hauling
teak logs

Dhoti
(loincloth)

Ox cart

VICTORIA
MEMORIAL

DHAKA

BANGLADESH

BURMA
(MYANMAR)

Opium
poppy

I A

Tiger

Coal

Rice

Calcutta

Mandalay

LINGARAJA
TEMPLE

PAGAN TEMPLE
(ANANDA)

Leg
rower

Tobacco

Fishing

BANGLADESH

"Giraffe"
necked woman
of Padaung

Hindu
dancer

NEPAL

SHWE
DAGON
PADOGA

T H A I L A N D

Krishna

BHUTAN

RANGOON
(YANGON)

Buddhist
monks

Mackerel

B A Y   O F   B E N G A L

BURMA (MYANMAR)

Rubber
trees

Madras

ANDAMAN
ISLANDS
(INDIA)

Lobster

Outrigger
fishing boat

SRI LANKA

Picking tea

Coconut
palms

SRI LANKA

COLOMBO

NICOBAR ISLANDS
(INDIA)

AFGHANISTAN
Capital: Kabul
Area: 652,090 sq km (251,792 sq miles)
Population: 17,375,000

BANGLADESH
Capital: Dhaka
Area: 143,998 sq km (55,602 sq miles)
Population: 108,851,000

BHUTAN
Capital: Thimphu
Area: 47,000 sq km (18,148 sq miles)
Population: 1,373,000

BURMA (MYANMAR)
Capital: Rangoon (Yangon)
Area: 676,552 sq km (261,237 sq miles)
Population: 40,162,000

INDIA
Capital: New Delhi
Area: 3,287,590 sq km (1,269,437 sq miles)
Population: 813,990,000

NEPAL
Capital: Kathmandu
Area: 140,797 sq km (54,365 sq miles)
Population: 18,053,000

PAKISTAN
Capital: Islamabad
Area: 796,095 sq km (307,396 sq miles)
Population: 105,677,000

SRI LANKA
Capital: Colombo
Area: 65,610 sq km (25,334 sq miles)
Population: 16,565,000

SOUTHEASTERN ASIA

SOUTHEASTERN ASIA is made up of a narrow strip of mainland and thousands of islands. The country of Indonesia consists of over 13,000 islands and has the fifth largest population in the world. Most Indonesians live on the island of Java. The Philippines is a collection of more than 7,000 islands. In contrast to these scatterings of islands is the tiny oil-rich country of Brunei. The Sultan (ruler) of Brunei is said to be the richest person in the world.

The climate in this region is hot and wet throughout the year, with very heavy rains during the monsoon season. Thick forests cover much of the area, though many trees have been cleared for timber and for growing crops such as rice, tobacco, pineapples, and rubber.

From the 16th–19th centuries most of the region was colonized by Europeans. This century many wars were fought between the local people and the colonizing countries, and today all the countries are independent again.

LAOS

THAILAND

CHINA

Cyclists

HANOI   Haiphong

THIEN MU PAGODA

Sampan

SOUTH CHINA SEA

BURMA (MYANMAR)

Mekong

Elephant hauling teak logs

Chao Phraya

Rice

VIENTIANE

LAOS

VIETNAM

Hue
Da Nang

THAILAND

Folk dancer

ANGKOR WAT

BANGKOK

CAMBODIA

PHNOM PENH

Rubber trees

Floating market

NHA TRANG BUDDHA
Ho Chi Minh City

Gas

Water buffalo

CAMBODIA   BRUNEI

Pearls

VIETNAM

Tourism

Phuket   Tin

Bananas

Rubber trees

Leatherback turtle

Freighter

Oil

Ambarita house

Tourism   Ipoh

MALAYSIA

MALAYSIA

Medan

Tin

Rubber trees

KUALA LUMPUR

Bandar Seri Begawan

BRUNEI

SARAWAK

Johor Baharu
SINGAPORE

Rubber trees

Pontianak

BORNEO

Timber

Orang-utan

Oil

SUMATRA

Oil

Padang

Oil

Flying fish

INDIAN OCEAN

"Perahu" fishing boat

Tiger

Pepper

Coconuts

Rice

Banjarmasin

Giant flowers (Rafflesia arnoldii)

Coffee

JAVA SEA

Javan rhinoceros

JAKARTA

BOROBUDUR TEMPLE

IND

SINGAPORE

SINGAPORE

Bandung   JAVA   Surabaya

INDONESIA

Malang   BALI

Tourism

Sail fish

COCOS ISLANDS
(Australia)

CHRISTMAS ISLAND
(Australia)

| 0 | 200 | 400 | 600 | 800 Kilometres |

| 0 | 100 | 200 | 300 | 400 | 500 Miles |

13 14 15 16 17 18 19 20 21 22 23

FACTS AND FIGURES

Planting rice in Malaysia. Seedlings are transplanted to a flooded field after they have grown in a nursery.

Longest river:
Mekong, 4,184 km (2,600 miles).

Longest name in the world:
The Thai name for Bangkok is Krungthep maha nakorn, amarn rattanakosindra, mahindrayudhya, mahadilok pop noparatana rajdhani mahasathan, amorn piman avatarn satit, sakkatultiya visanukarn prasit.

Largest cities:
Jakarta (Indonesia), 7,829,000; Manila (Philippines), 5,926,000; Bangkok (Thailand), 5,609,000; Ho Chi Minh City (Vietnam, previously called Saigon), 4,000,000.

Highest mountain: Puncak Jaya (Indonesia), 5,030 m (16,503 ft).

Largest island: New Guinea, 808,510 sq km (312,085 sq miles).

BRUNEI
Capital: Bandar Seri Begawan
Area: 5,765 sq km (2,225 sq miles)
Population: 243,000
Languages: Malay, English
Religion: Moslem

CAMBODIA
Capital: Phnom Pénh
Area: 181,035 sq km (69,881 sq miles)
Population: 5,728,771
Language: Khmer
Religion: Buddhist

INDONESIA
Capital: Jakarta
Area: 1,904,569 sq km (735,412 sq miles)
Population: 17-,832,000
Language: Indonesian
Religion: Moslem

LAOS
Capital: Vientiane
Area: 236,800 sq km (91,435 sq miles)
Population: 3,379,000
Languages: Lao, French
Religion: Buddhist

MALAYSIA
Capital: Kuala Lumpur
Area: 329,749 sq km (127,326 sq miles)
Population: 15,921,000
Languages: Malay, English, Chinese
Religions: Moslem, Buddhist

PAPUA NEW GUINEA
Capital: Port Moresby
Area: 462,840 sq km (178,716 sq miles)
Population: 3,804,000
Languages: English, numerous others
Religion: Christian

PHILIPPINES
Capital: Manila
Area: 300,000 sq km (115,839 sq miles)
Population: 59,686,000
Languages: Pilipino, English, Spanish
Religions: Christian, Moslem

SINGAPORE
Capital: Singapore City
Area: 618 sq km (239 sq miles)
Population: 2,639,000
Languages: Malay, Chinese, English
Religions: Taoist, Buddhist

THAILAND
Capital: Bangkok
Area: 513,115 sq km (198,129 sq miles)
Population: 54,469,000
Language: Thai
Religion: Buddhist

VIETNAM
Capital: Hanoi
Area: 329,558 sq km (127,252 sq miles)
Population: 66,682,000
Languages: Vietnamese, French, Chinese
Religion: Buddhist

SINGAPORE

Singapore is a small island, just 40 km (25 miles) long by 25 km (15.5 miles) wide. It is an independent nation and one of the world's most important ports and trading centres. Many different races live in Singapore. Three-quarters of the population are Chinese, with smaller numbers of Malays and Indians. The remainder are Europeans, Arabs, or Japanese. These people all celebrate different festivals, making Singapore a lively and colourful place throughout the year.

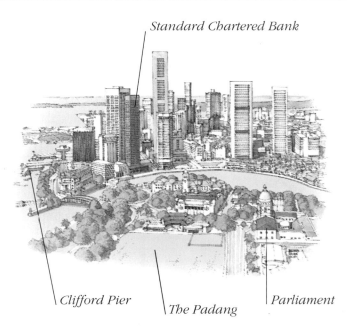

Standard Chartered Bank

Clifford Pier   The Padang   Parliament

TAIWAN

PACIFIC OCEAN

MANILA
LUZON
Rice terraces

PHILIPPINES

Sugar cane

●Cebu

PHILIPPINES

Coral reefs

Monkey-eating eagle

MINDANAO
●Davao
Zamboanga

Vinta boat
Coral reefs

CELEBES SEA

Coconuts

Sago palms

MOLUCCAS   Oil
Shrimps   Nutmeg   Oil

Toraja House

SERAM SEA
SERAM

CELEBES

Cloves

Coffee

Crabs

BANDA SEA

●**Ujung Pandang**

ONESIA

Komodo dragon

FLORES
Maize
SUMBA   TIMOR
●Kupang

TIMOR SEA

ARAFURA SEA

AUSTRALIA

Sago palms

Tuna

Jayapura●

IRIAN JAYA
△ Puncak Jaya
5,030 m

Tree kangaroo

Irian Jaya native

Asmat warriors

Bird of paradise

Spirit house

Coconuts

NEW BRITAIN

PAPUA NEW GUINEA
△ Mt Wilhelm 4,508 m

PAPUA

Dancer and drum

PORT MORESBY●

PAPUA NEW GUINEA

13 14 15 16 17 18 19 20 21 22 23

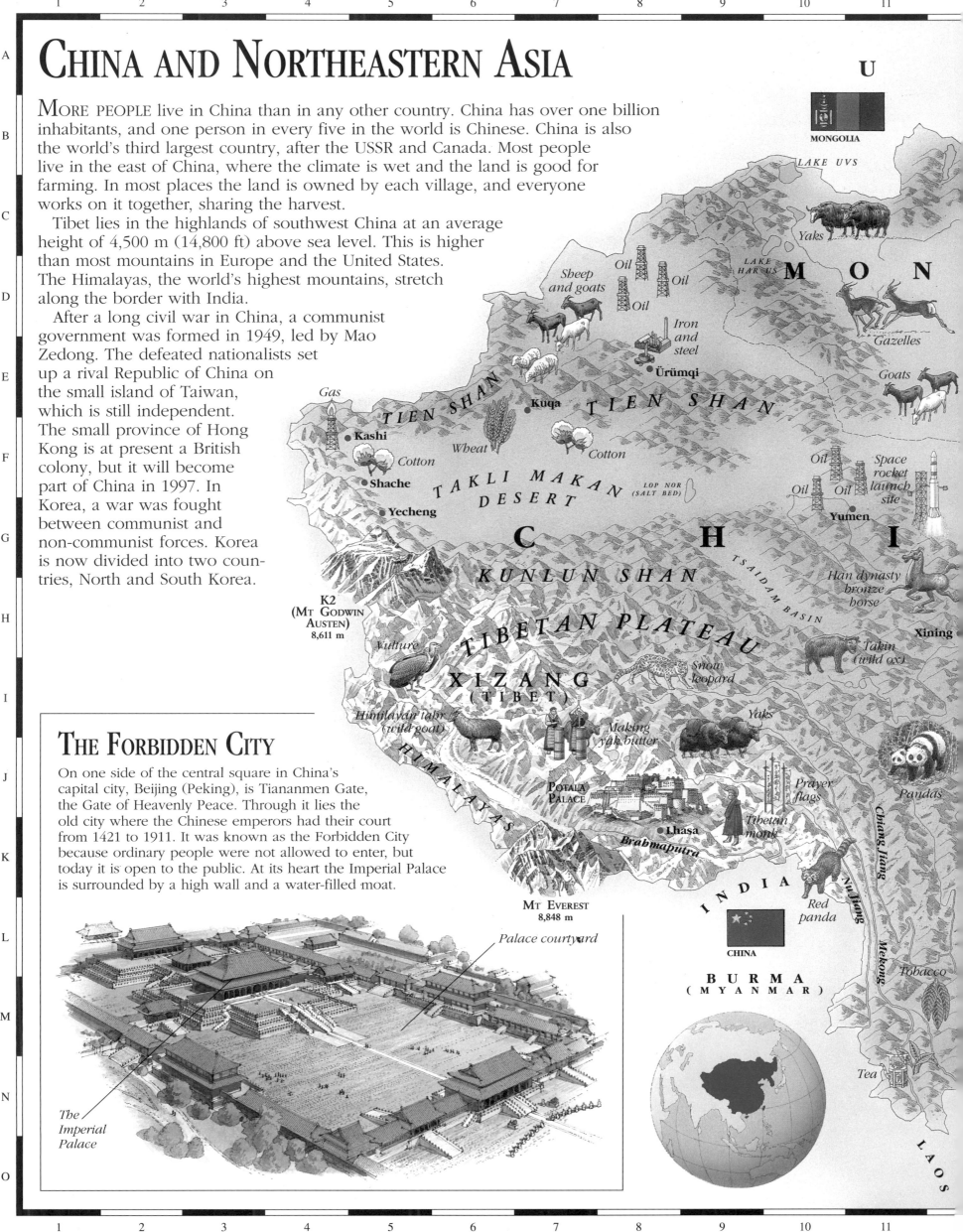

CHINA AND NORTHEASTERN ASIA

MORE PEOPLE live in China than in any other country. China has over one billion inhabitants, and one person in every five in the world is Chinese. China is also the world's third largest country, after the USSR and Canada. Most people live in the east of China, where the climate is wet and the land is good for farming. In most places the land is owned by each village, and everyone works on it together, sharing the harvest.

Tibet lies in the highlands of southwest China at an average height of 4,500 m (14,800 ft) above sea level. This is higher than most mountains in Europe and the United States. The Himalayas, the world's highest mountains, stretch along the border with India.

After a long civil war in China, a communist government was formed in 1949, led by Mao Zedong. The defeated nationalists set up a rival Republic of China on the small island of Taiwan, which is still independent. The small province of Hong Kong is at present a British colony, but it will become part of China in 1997. In Korea, a war was fought between communist and non-communist forces. Korea is now divided into two countries, North and South Korea.

THE FORBIDDEN CITY

On one side of the central square in China's capital city, Beijing (Peking), is Tiananmen Gate, the Gate of Heavenly Peace. Through it lies the old city where the Chinese emperors had their court from 1421 to 1911. It was known as the Forbidden City because ordinary people were not allowed to enter, but today it is open to the public. At its heart the Imperial Palace is surrounded by a high wall and a water-filled moat.

Palace courtyard

The Imperial Palace

MONGOLIA

U

LAKE UVS

Yaks

M O N

LAKE HAR US

Sheep and goats

Oil
Oil
Oil

Iron and steel

Ürümqi

Gazelles

Goats

Gas

TIEN SHAN

Kashi

Kuqa

TIEN SHAN

Cotton

Wheat

Cotton

Shache

TAKLI MAKAN DESERT

LOP NOR (SALT BED)

Oil

Oil   Oil

Space rocket launch site

Yecheng

C H I

Yumen

Han dynasty bronze horse

TSAIDAM BASIN

KUNLUN SHAN

K2 (MT GODWIN AUSTEN) 8,611 m

Vulture

TIBETAN PLATEAU

Xining

Takin (wild ox)

XIZANG (TIBET)

Snow leopard

Himalayan tahr (wild goat)

Yaks

HIMALAYAS

Making yak butter

Pandas

POTALA PALACE

Prayer flags

Lhasa

Tibetan monk

Brahmaputra

Chiang Jiang

MT EVEREST 8,848 m

INDIA

CHINA

Red panda

Nu Jiang

BURMA (MYANMAR)

Mekong

Tobacco

Tea

LAOS

S S R

MONGOLIA

Sheep

ULAN BATOR

G O L I A

Cowboy and wild horse

Gers (Mongol tents)

G O B I   D E S E R T

Bactrian camels

INNER MONGOLIA

LAKE HULUN

Kaoliang (cereal crop)

Qiqihar

Coal

Songhua

Coal

Vehicles

Oil

Harbin

Tiger

Oil

Soya beans

Vehicles

Jilin

Changchun

Liao

Iron and steel

Goats

TEMPLE OF HEAVEN

Wheat

Coal

Shenyang

Fushun

NORTH KOREA

Maize

Diesel locomotives

Anshan

Locomotives

Iron and steel

Baotou

GREAT WALL OF CHINA

C H I N A

BEIJING (PEKING)

Dalian

PYONGYANG

Shipbuilding

Electronics and vehicles

Yinchuan

Sheep

Cyclists

Tianjin

SEOUL

SOUTH KOREA

Wuwei

Oil

YELLOW SEA

SEA OF JAPAN

Taiyuan

Maize

Jinan

Fish

Millet

Cotton

Iron and steel

Qingdao

Fish

Shipbuilding

KOREA STRAIT

NORTH KOREA

Lanzhou

TERRACOTTA ARMY

Vehicles

Huang He

Wheat

SOUTH KOREA

Chemicals and textiles

Luoyang

Zhengzhou

Planting rice

Xi'an

Sweet potatoes

Ducks

Porcelain

Tobacco

Chang Jiang

Shipbuilding

Oil

Oil

Yun Xian

Iron and steel

Nanjing

Cotton

Shanghai

Fish

Maize

Cotton

Chengdu

Wuhan

Hangzhou

Fishing

Chang Jiang

Rice

EAST CHINA SEA

Millet

Nan Xian

Goldfish

Chongqing

Nanchang

Wenzhou

Chemicals and vehicles

Junk

Tea

Changsha

Silk

Nanping

Limestone hills

Sweet potatoes

Guiyang

Pigs

Ganzhou

Fuzhou

Water buffalo plough

Planting rice

Sugar cane

T'AIPEI

Kunming

Guilin

Liuzhou

Sampan

TAIWAN

PHILIPPINE SEA

Mengzi

Pigs

Guangzhou (Canton)

Malipo

Shantou

Nanning

Chaoyang

Skyscrapers of modern Hong Kong

V I E T N A M

Sugar cane

HONG KONG

MACAU

Shellfish

Gibbon

Junk fishing

Rubber trees

HAINAN

SOUTH CHINA SEA

NORTH KOREA

SOUTH KOREA

TAIWAN

0   200   400   600   800 Kilometres

0   100   200   300   400   500 Miles

FACTS AND FIGURES

The Great Wall of China was built to protect the country's northern border against invaders. It is nearly 3,460 km (2,150 miles) long.

Longest river:
Chang Jiang (Yangste). 6,300 km (3,915 miles).

Largest city population:
Shanghai (China), 12,320,000.

Gateway to the Chaotain Palace, one of many historic buildings in Nanjing, formerly the capital of China.

CHINA
Capital: Beijing (Peking)
Area: 9,596,961 sq km (3,704,440 sq miles)
Population: 1,083,889,000
Languages: Chinese
Religions: Confucianism, Buddhism, Taoism, Moslem
Currency: Yuan
Government: Communist republic

HONG KONG
Capital: Victoria
Area: 1,045 sq km (403 sq miles)
Population: 5,674,000
Languages: English and Chinese
Religions: Buddhism, Christianity, Taoism
Currency: Hong Kong dollar
Government: British colony

MACAU
Capital: Macau
Area: 16 sq km (6 sq miles)
Population: 443,000
Languages: Portuguese and Chinese
Religions: Buddhism, Christianity, Taoism
Currency: Pataca
Government: Portuguese colony

MONGOLIA
Capital: Ulan Bator
Area: 1,565,000 sq km (604,247 sq miles)
Population: 2,086,000
Language: Mongolian
Religions: Buddhism, Lamaism, Moslem
Currency: Tugrik
Government: Communist republic

NORTH KOREA
Capital: Pyongyang
Area: 120,538 sq km (46,540 sq miles)
Population: 21,877,000
Language: Korean
Religions: Buddhism, Confucianism, Taoism
Currency: Won
Government: Communist republic

SOUTH KOREA
Capital: Seoul
Area: 99,016 sq km (38,230 sq miles)
Population: 42,593,000
Language: Korean
Religions: Buddhism, Christianity, Confucianism
Currency: Won
Government: Republic

TAIWAN
Capital: T'aipei
Area: 35,990 sq km (13,890 sq miles)
Population: 19,700,000
Language: Chinese
Religions: Buddhism, Taoism, Christianity
Currency: New Taiwan dollar
Government: Republic

JAPAN

JAPAN is made up of four main islands – called Hokkaido, Honshu, Shikoku, and Kyushu – and thousands of smaller ones. The country lies to the east of the main part of Asia. This is an area where two plates of the Earth's crust meet, making earthquakes common. Nearly three-quarters of the country is mountainous and wooded. There is little land suitable for agriculture, but what there is is farmed very efficiently. The main crop is rice. Because much of the land cannot be farmed for food, the Japanese eat a lot of fish, and Japan catches more fish than any other nation.

Japan's 122 million people live on the small amount of flat land, mostly on the coasts. In these populated areas there is a very dense concentration of people and activity. Most of the people live in the great cities on the south coast of Honshu island, such as Nagoya, Tokyo, and Osaka.

In the last 40 years Japan has become one of the world's most important industrial nations. This is all the more remarkable because the oil and most of the raw materials that are needed to make the goods have to be imported into the country. Japanese cars, electrical goods, ships, cameras, and many other products are exported all over the world.

KYOTO

Kyoto (or Heian) lies on the island of Honshu. It is one of Japan's largest cities and an important cultural centre. For more than 1,000 years it was the capital city of Japan. It has many historic treasures, including shrines, temples, gardens, and ancient buildings. It is Japan's most popular tourist centre and about 20 million people visit the city every year.

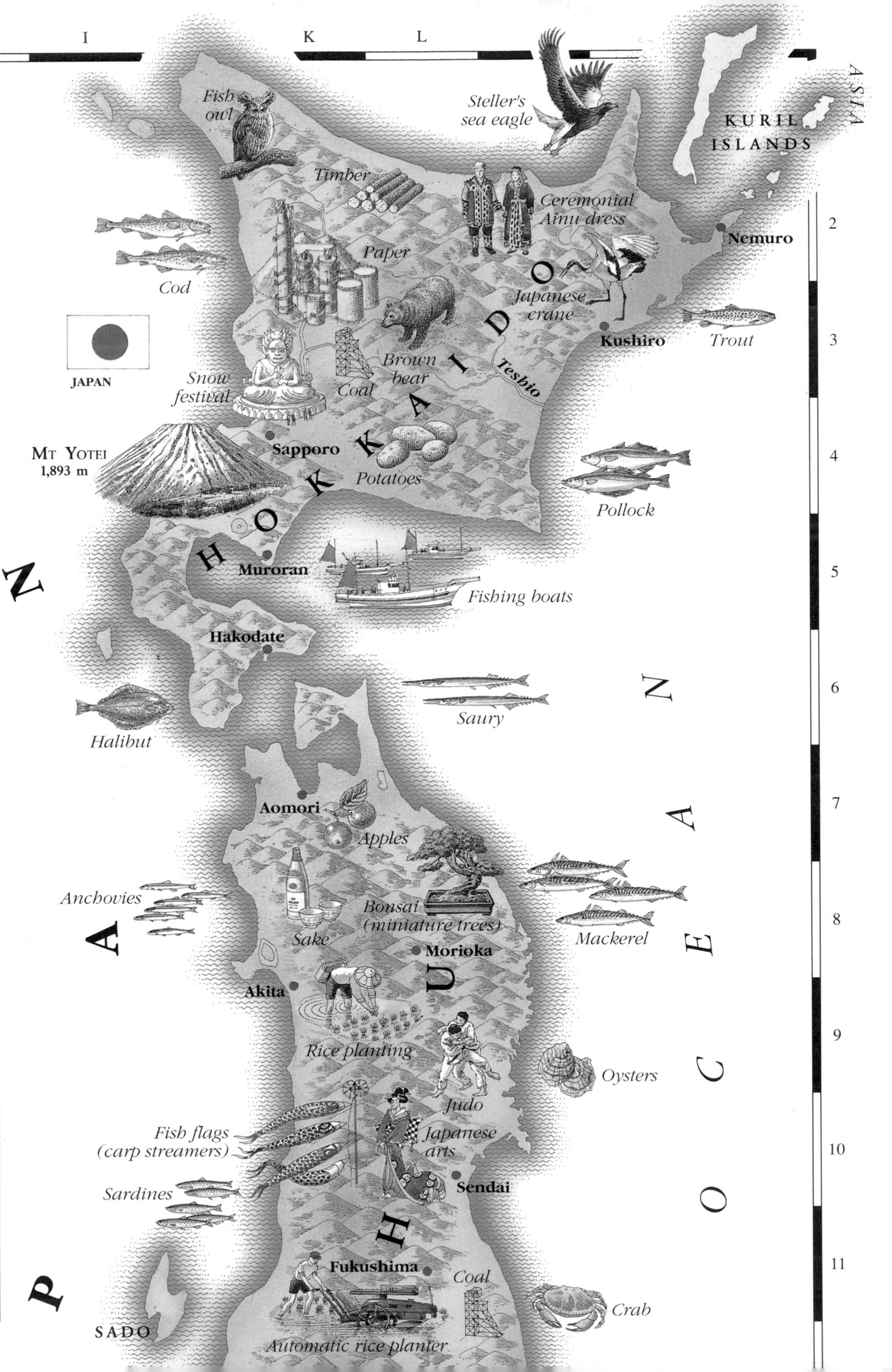

Map labels

KURIL ISLANDS

Nemuro
Trout
Kushiro
Pollock
Ceremonial Ainu dress
Japanese crane
Steller's sea eagle
Teshio
HOKKAIDO
Timber
Paper
Brown bear
Coal
Potatoes
Fish oil
Cod
Snow festival
Sapporo
Muroran
Hakodate
MT YOTEI 1,893 m
Fishing boats
Saury
Halibut

JAPAN

Anchovies
Aomori
Apples
Sake
Akita
Bonsai (miniature trees)
Morioka
Judo
Rice planting
Japanese arts
Sendai
Oysters
Mackerel
Crab
Fukushima
Coal
Automatic rice planter
Fish flags (carp streamers)
Sardines
SADO
HONSHU

PACIFIC OCEAN

SEA OF JAPAN

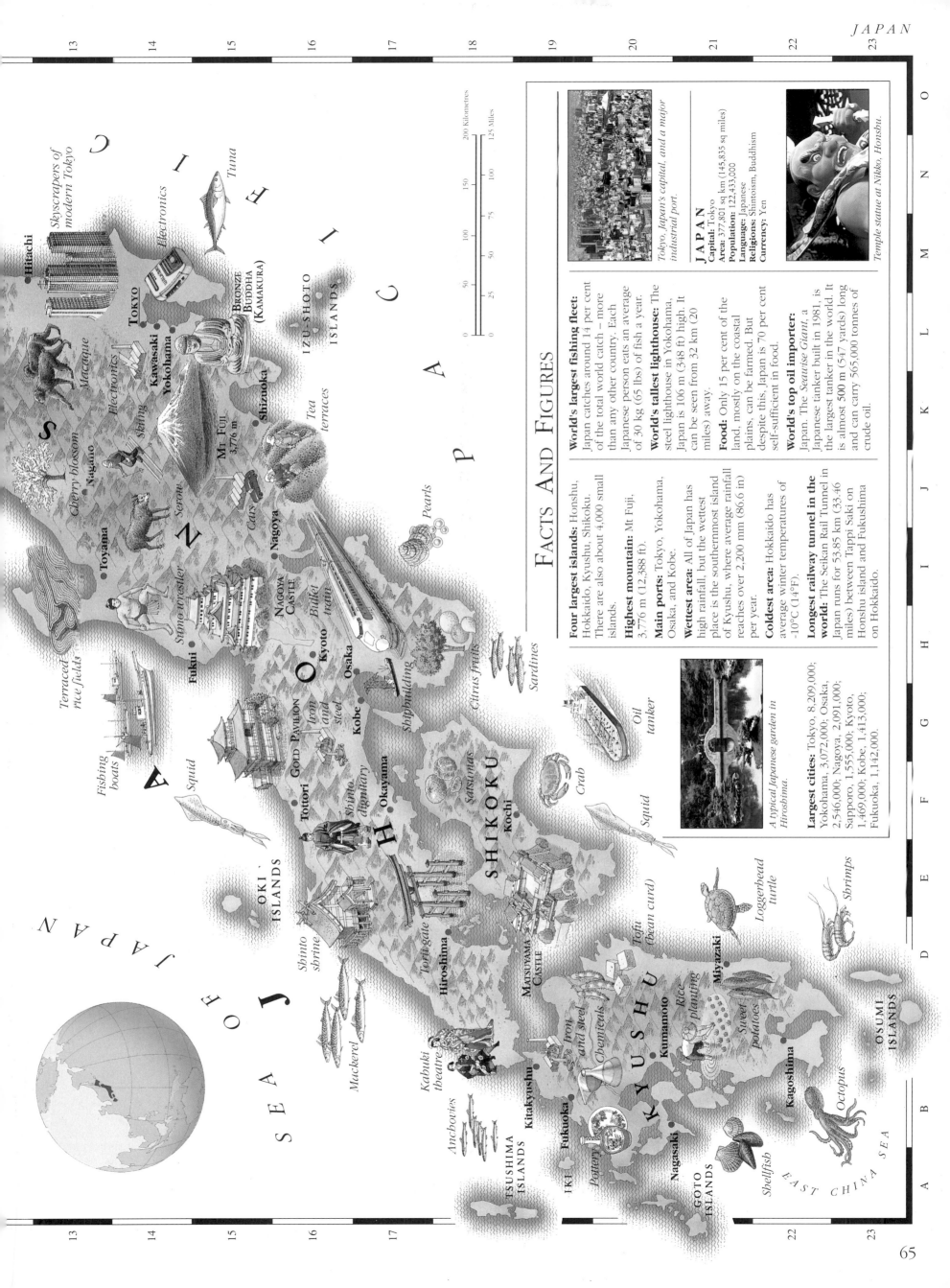

JAPAN

Capital: Tokyo
Area: 377,801 sq km (145,835 sq miles)
Population: 122,433,000
Language: Japanese
Religions: Shintoism, Buddhism
Currency: Yen

Tokyo, Japan's capital, and a major industrial port.

Temple statue at Nikko, Honshu.

FACTS AND FIGURES

Four largest islands: Honshu, Hokkaido, Kyushu, Shikoku. There are also about 4,000 small islands.

Highest mountain: Mt Fuji, 3,776 m (12,388 ft).

Main ports: Tokyo, Yokohama, Osaka, and Kobe.

Wettest area: All of Japan has high rainfall, but the wettest place is the southernmost island of Kyushu, where average rainfall reaches over 2,200 mm (86.6 in) per year.

Coldest area: Hokkaido has average winter temperatures of -10°C (14°F).

Longest railway tunnel in the world: The Seikan Rail Tunnel in Japan runs for 53.85 km (33.46 miles) between Tappi Saki on Honshu island and Fukushima on Hokkaido.

World's largest fishing fleet: Japan catches around 14 per cent of the total world catch – more than any other country. Each Japanese person eats an average of 30 kg (65 lbs) of fish a year.

World's tallest lighthouse: The steel lighthouse in Yokohama, Japan is 106 m (348 ft) high. It can be seen from 32 km (20 miles) away.

Food: Only 15 per cent of the land, mostly on the coastal plains, can be farmed. But despite this, Japan is 70 per cent self-sufficient in food.

World's top oil importer: Japan. The *Seawise Giant*, a Japanese tanker built in 1981, is the largest tanker in the world. It is almost 500 m (547 yards) long and can carry 565,000 tonnes of crude oil.

A typical Japanese garden in Hiroshima.

Largest cities: Tokyo, 8,209,000; Yokohama, 3,072,000; Osaka, 2,546,000; Nagoya, 2,091,000; Sapporo, 1,555,000; Kyoto, 1,469,000; Kobe, 1,413,000; Fukuoka, 1,142,000.

Map labels:

Skyscrapers of modern Tokyo
Hitachi
Electronics
Tuna
Macaque
TOKYO
Electronics
Kawasaki
Yokohama
Cherry blossom
Nagano
Skiing
Shizuoka
BRONZE BUDDHA (KAMAKURA)
IZU-SHOTO ISLANDS
Serow
Mt FUJI 3,776 m
Tea terraces
Toyama
Sumo wrestler
Cars
Nagoya
Pearls
Terraced rice fields
Fukui
NAGOYA CASTLE
Bullet train
Kyoto
Iron and steel
GOLD PAVILION
Osaka
Kobe
Shipbuilding
Citrus fruits
Sardines
Fishing boats
Squid
Tottori
Shinto dignitary
Okayama
Satsumas
SHIKOKU
Kochi
Crab
Squid
Oil tanker
SEA OF JAPAN
OKI ISLANDS
Shinto shrine
Torii gate
Hiroshima
MATSUYAMA CASTLE
Tofu (bean curd)
Loggerhead turtle
Shrimps
Mackerel
Kabuki theatre
Iron and steel
Chemicals
Kumamoto
Rice planting
Miyazaki
Sweet potatoes
TSUSHIMA ISLANDS
Anchovies
Kitakyushu
Fukuoka
Pottery
Nagasaki
GOTO ISLANDS
Shellfish
KYUSHU
Kagoshima
Octopus
OSUMI ISLANDS
EAST CHINA SEA

Scale: 200 Kilometres / 125 Miles

AFRICA

The Muhammad Ali mosque in Cairo, Egypt.

AFRICA, the world's second largest continent, stretches about 4,000 km (2,500 miles) north and south of the Equator. It is the warmest of all the continents. The only permanent snow and ice are found on the peaks of the highest mountains, such as Mount Kenya and Mount Kilimanjaro. In the regions near the Equator, the hot and wet climate supports the dense jungle vegetation of the tropical rainforest. Today much of the forest has been cleared for farming and timber.

Moving away from the Equator, the climate becomes increasingly dry, and the forest gives way to tropical grassland, called savannah. For thousands of years the savannah has supported huge herds of plant-eating animals – gazelles, wildebeest, zebras, elephants, and giraffes – along with the predators who hunt and feed on them – lions, leopards, and hyenas. Today farming has greatly reduced the size of the herds, and some animals, such as the African elephant, are in danger of being wiped out forever.

Still farther to the north and south lie the great deserts, where the climate is so dry that few plants

Open cast mining in South Africa.

and animals can survive. Northern Africa is dominated by the Sahara, the world's largest desert. In the south lie the Kalahari and Namib deserts.

Africa is an immense plateau, broken by a few mountain ranges. In some areas a narrow coastal plain stretches along the edge of the plateau. Cutting across East Africa is the Great Rift Valley, with its many lakes and volcanoes. This long valley was formed centuries ago when land slipped down between huge cracks in the Earth's crust. Some scientists believe that the land east of the Rift Valley will eventually break away from Africa and become a new continent, just as the Red Sea marks the place where Arabia once split away from the rest of Africa.

Off the east coast of Africa lies the island of Madagascar, which broke away from Africa over 50 million years ago. Because of the island's isolation, unique plants and animals have evolved there. Twenty species of lemur, an animal distantly related to the monkey, are only found there.

Equatorial vegetation in Cameroon.

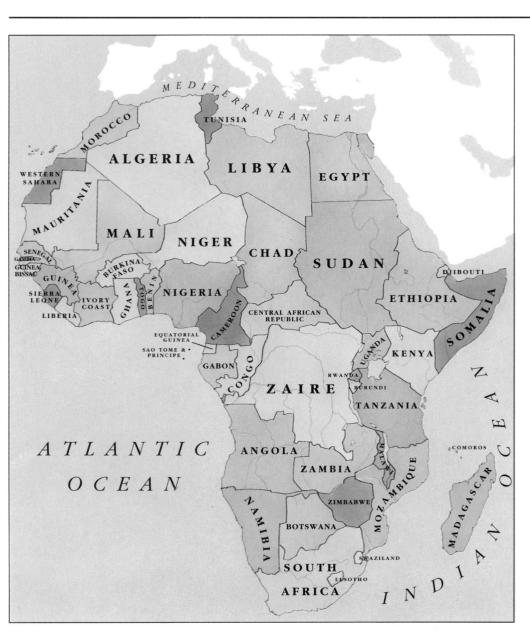

FACTS ABOUT AFRICA

Area: 30,335,000 sq km (11,712,434 sq miles).

Population: 613,566,000.

Number of independent countries: 52 (the most on any continent).

Largest countries: Sudan, 2,500,000 sq km (967,5000 sq miles); Algeria, 2,381,741 sq km (919, 597 sq miles).

Most populated countries: Nigeria, 110,131,000; Egypt, 51,447,000; Ethiopia, 46,144,000.

Largest cities: Cairo (Egypt), 6,325,000; Alexandria (Egypt), 2,893,000; Kinshasa (Zaire), 2,653,000.

Highest mountains: Kilimanjaro (Tanzania), 5,896 m (19,344 ft); Mt Kenya (Kenya), 5,199 m (17,057 ft); Mt Margherita (Uganda-Zaire), 5,110 m (16,763 ft); Ras Dashen (Ethiopia), 4,620 m (15,158 ft).

Longest rivers: Nile, 6,670 km (4,145 miles), the longest in the world; Zaire, 4,667 km (2,900 miles); Niger, 4,184 km (2,600 miles); Zambezi, 2,735 km (1,700 miles).

Largest lakes: Lake Victoria, 69,400 sq km (26,800 sq miles); Lake Tanganyika, 32,900 sq km (12,102 sq miles); Lake Nyasa, 28,750 sq km (11,100 sq miles); Lake Chad, area varies from 10,000-26,000 sq km (4,000-10,000 sq miles), according to the seasons.

Main deserts: Sahara (the largest in the world), about 9,000,000 sq km (3,474,927 sq miles); Kalahari, about 517,998 sq km (200,000 sq miles).

Largest islands: Madagascar, 587,041 sq km (226,658 sq miles); Socotra, 3,579 sq km (1,382 sq miles); Réunion, 2,510 sq km (969 sq miles).

World's highest sand dunes: Dunes in the Sahara Desert can be up to 5 km (3 miles) long and 430 m (1,410 ft) high.

World's highest temperature: In 1922 the temperature in Al'Azizya (Libya) reached 58°C (136.4°F) in the shade.

World's largest man-made lake: Lake Volta (Ghana), which was formed by the Akosombo Dam, covers an area of 8,482 sq km (3,275 miles).

13 14 15 16 17 18 19 20 21 22 23

A
B
C
D

ATLANTIC

EUROPE

ASIA

STRAIT OF GIBRALTAR

MEDITERRANEAN SEA

GULF OF SIRTE

MADEIRA

ATLAS MTS

△ JEBEL
TOUBKAL
4,165 m

CANARY
ISLANDS

S A H A R A

LAKE
NASSER

NUBIAN
DESERT

ARABIAN
PENINSULA

RED SEA

ARABIAN
SEA

*AHAGGAR
MTS*

*AIR
MASSIF*

*TIBESTI
MASSIF*

Niger

Nile

Nile

Atbara

Blue Nile

△ RAS DASHEN
4,620 m

GULF OF ADEN

SOCOTRA

CAPE
VERDE
ISLANDS

Senegal

Gambia

LAKE
CHAD

S A H E L

Benue

LAKE
VOLTA

Niger

GULF OF
GUINEA

BIOKO

Zaire

White Nile

LAKE
TURKANA

GREAT RIFT VALLEY

△ MT CAMEROON
4,100 m

PRINCIPE·
SÃO TOMÉ

MT MARGHERITA △
5,110 m

△ MT KENYA
5,199 m

SEYCHELLES

LAKE
MAI-NDOMBE

LAKE
VICTORIA

△ MT KILIMANJARO
5,896 m

Zaire

Lualaba

LAKE
TANGANYIKA

ZANZIBAR

ASCENSION

GREAT RIFT VALLEY

LAKE
NYASA

COMOROS

Zambezi

MADAGASCAR

LAKE
KARIBA

*MOZAMBIQUE
CHANNEL*

ST HELENA

Okavango

Limpopo

MAURITIUS
RÉUNION

NAMIB DESERT

KALAHARI
DESERT

DRAKENSBERG

Orange

INDIAN

ATLANTIC

OCEAN

OCEAN

CAPE OF
GOOD HOPE

TRISTAN DA
CUNHA

L
M
N
O

13 14 15 16 17 18 19 20 21 22 23

NORTHERN AFRICA

DOMINATING NORTHERN AFRICA is the huge expanse of the Sahara Desert. The climate is wetter along parts of the north coasts, and here citrus fruits, grapes, and dates are grown. Along the Mediterranean coastline tourism is increasingly important. The largest countries in Northern Africa are Egypt, a farming country, and Libya and Algeria, which have rich supplies of oil and natural gas.

The few people who live in the Sahara Desert are mostly nomads, who move from place to place with their sheep and camels. Along the southern edge of the Sahara is an area of semi-desert called the Sahel, which stretches across the countries of Mauritania, Niger, Chad, and Mali. These are among the world's poorest countries. In recent years the people there have suffered terrible famines.

West Africa, which includes the countries of Nigeria, Ghana, Benin and Ivory Coast, is a fertile region in which such crops as coffee, groundnuts, and cocoa are grown.

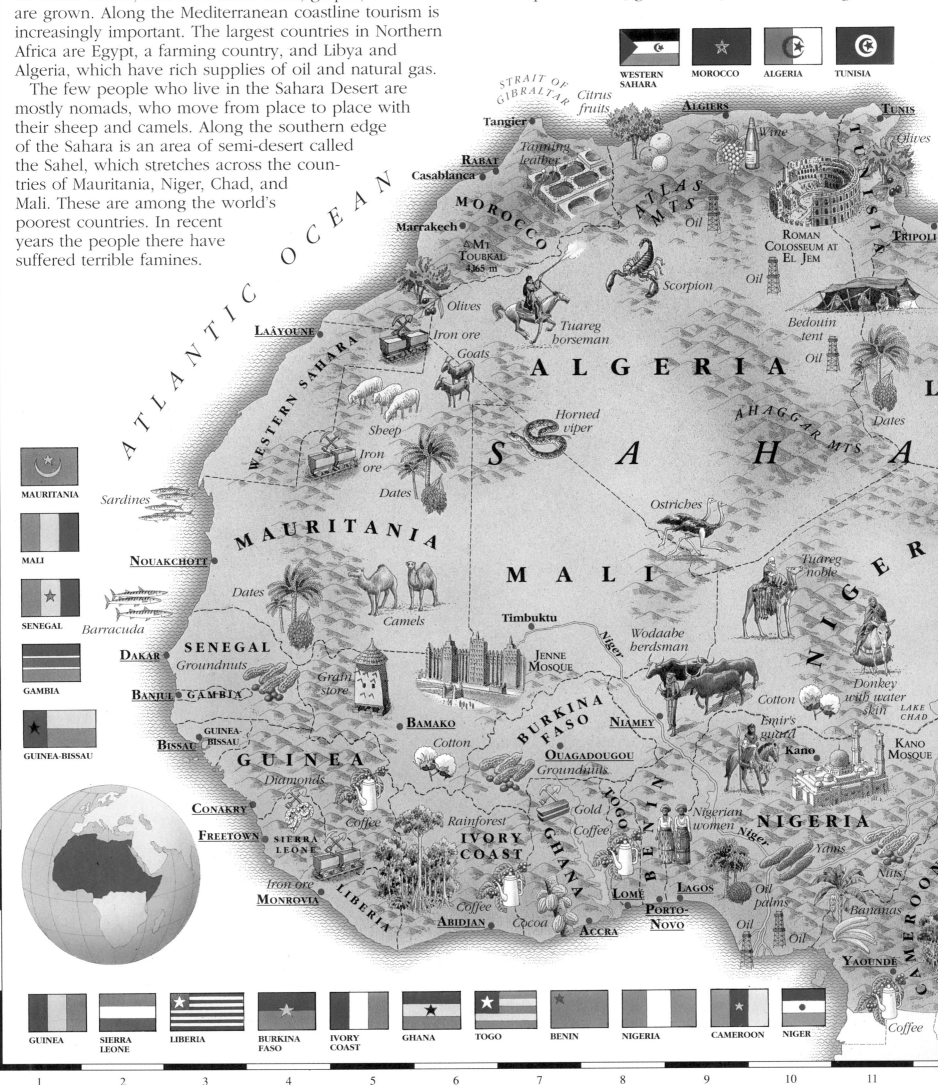

WESTERN SAHARA   MOROCCO   ALGERIA   TUNISIA

MAURITANIA

MALI

SENEGAL

GAMBIA

GUINEA-BISSAU

GUINEA   SIERRA LEONE   LIBERIA   BURKINA FASO   IVORY COAST   GHANA   TOGO   BENIN   NIGERIA   CAMEROON   NIGER

STRAIT OF GIBRALTAR
Citrus fruits
Tangier
Rabat
Casablanca
Marrakech
MOROCCO
ATLAS MTS
Wine
ALGIERS
TUNIS
TUNISIA
Olives
Oil
ROMAN COLOSSEUM AT EL JEM
Scorpion
Oil
TRIPOLI
Mt Toubkal 4,165 m
Olives
Iron ore
Tuareg horseman
Goats
ALGERIA
Horned viper
AHAGGAR MTS
Dates
Bedouin tent
Oil
LAÂYOUNE
WESTERN SAHARA
Sheep
Iron ore
Dates
SAHARA
Ostriches
ATLANTIC OCEAN
Sardines
MAURITANIA
Dates
Camels
MALI
Timbuktu
Tuareg noble
NIGER
NOUAKCHOTT
Barracuda
SENEGAL
DAKAR
Groundnuts
Grain store
JENNE MOSQUE
Wodaabe herdsman
Donkey with water skin
LAKE CHAD
BANJUL   GAMBIA
BAMAKO
Cotton
BURKINA FASO
NIAMEY
Cotton
Emir's guard
BISSAU
GUINEA-BISSAU
Cotton
OUAGADOUGOU
Groundnuts
KANO
KANO MOSQUE
CONAKRY
GUINEA
Diamonds
Gold
Coffee
Nigerian women
NIGERIA
FREETOWN
SIERRA LEONE
Coffee
Rainforest
IVORY COAST
GHANA
BENIN
Yams
Iron ore
LIBERIA
Coffee
TOGO
LOMÉ
Oil palms
Nuts
MONROVIA
Cocoa
LAGOS
Oil
ABIDJAN
ACCRA
PORTO-NOVO
Oil
Bananas
CAMEROON
YAOUNDÉ
Coffee

THE PYRAMIDS AND SPHINX

The pyramids of ancient Egypt were built in about 2500 BC to contain the mummified bodies of pharaohs, or kings. The three largest are at Giza. The Great Pyramid contains more than two million stone blocks. The Sphinx was probably built to guard the Pharaoh Chephren's body.

Pyramid of Chephren

Great Pyramid of Cheops

Pyramid of Mycerinus

FACTS AND FIGURES

Port Said lies at the entrance to the Suez Canal which links the Mediterranean and Red Seas.

Longest river: Nile, 6,670 km (4,145 miles).

Highest mountains: Ras Dashen (Ethiopia), 4,620 m (15,158 ft); Mt Toubkal (Morocco), 4,165 m (13,664 ft).

Largest lake: Lake Chad, area varies from 10,000–26,000 sq km (4,000–10,000 sq miles) according to the season.

ALGERIA
Capital: Algiers

BENIN
Capital: Porto-Novo

BURKINA FASO
Capital: Ouagadougou

CAMEROON
Capital: Yaoundé

CENTRAL AFRICAN REPUBLIC
Capital: Bangui

CHAD
Capital: N'Djamena

DJIBOUTI
Capital: Djibouti

EGYPT
Capital: Cairo

ETHIOPIA
Capital: Addis Ababa

GAMBIA
Capital: Banjul

GHANA
Capital: Accra

GUINEA
Capital: Conakry

GUINEA-BISSAU
Capital: Bissau

IVORY COAST
Capital: Abidjan

LIBERIA
Capital: Monrovia

LIBYA
Capital: Tripoli

MALI
Capital: Bamako

MAURITANIA
Capital: Nouakchott

MOROCCO
Capital: Rabat

NIGER
Capital: Niamey

NIGERIA
Capital: Lagos

SENEGAL
Capital: Dakar

SIERRA LEONE
Capital: Freetown

SOMALIA
Capital: Mogadishu

SUDAN
Capital: Khartoum

TOGO
Capital: Lomé

TUNISIA
Capital: Tunis

WESTERN SAHARA
Capital: Laâyoune

MEDITERRANEAN SEA

Benghazi · Alexandria · Port Said · CAIRO · SINAI

Olives · Oil · Dates · Citrus fruits · PYRAMIDS AT GIZA · Oil

LIBYA · EGYPT

Dates · Jerboa · TIBESTI MASSIF · Striped hyena · Dates · Felucca (Egyptian boat) · LAKE NASSER · Cotton · Nile

THE GREAT TEMPLE AT ABU SIMBEL · Nile crocodile · NUBIAN DESERT · Port Sudan

PYRAMIDS AT MEROE

CHAD · SUDAN

Nomadic caravan · Dates · Ostriches · KHARTOUM · Coffee · RAS DASHEN 4,620 m

Hippopotami · Sugar cane · White Nile · Blue Nile · Nomadic tribesman

N'DJAMENA · Nuba five-turret dwelling

Groundnuts · Chari · Cheetah · Nuba tribesmen · ADDIS ABABA · Cotton · Frankincense (Boswellia tree)

Logone · Rhinoceros · ETHIOPIA · Goats

Cotton · CENTRAL AFRICAN REPUBLIC · Great white pelican · Oryx

Diamonds · Elephant · Thatched huts of the Nuer tribe · Acacia tree · SOMALIA

Rainforest · Lions · Giraffes

BANGUI · Lions · Bananas · MOGADISHU

RED SEA · GULF OF ADEN · Dhow (Arab boat) · DJIBOUTI · INDIAN OCEAN

CENTRAL AFRICAN REPUBLIC · CHAD · LIBYA · EGYPT · SUDAN · ETHIOPIA · DJIBOUTI · SOMALIA

SOUTHERN AFRICA

SOUTHERN AFRICA contains a great variety of peoples and landscapes. In the northwest lies the rainforest of the Zaire Basin. To the east lie the high grasslands of East Africa, where the peaks of Mt Kenya and Mt Kilimanjaro are snow-capped all year long and large herds of wild animals still roam the plains. The countries of Kenya, Uganda, and Tanzania contain rich farmland where coffee, tea, maize, and cotton are grown.

Angola, Zambia, and Zimbabwe are rich in diamonds, iron, and copper. Farther south lies the Kalahari Desert, which covers much of Botswana and Namibia. The world's richest diamond and gold mines are in South Africa. This country is also a major producer of fruit, wheat, cotton, and tobacco.

Until about 100 years ago Europeans called Africa the "Dark Continent", because they knew so little about its interior. Then they began to explore inland and claim areas as colonies. All of these have now been returned to the Africans except for South Africa. Under a system called apartheid, which means "separate development", South Africa's black population is governed by a small number of white people. This has caused considerable unrest and violence. In 1990 the government promised to end apartheid.

THE GREAT RIFT VALLEY

The Great Rift Valley is the largest crack in the Earth's crust, stretching 8,700 km (5,400 miles) from Syria in the north, through the Red Sea to Mozambique in southern Africa. It is in East Africa that the scenery of the Rift Valley is most spectacular. In Kenya the walls of the valley rise almost straight up for 1,250 m (4,000 ft).

EQUATORIAL GUINEA

GABON

CONGO

ZAIRE

ANGOLA

ZAMBIA

NAMIBIA

BOTSWANA

SOUTH AFRICA

NIGERIA

CAMEROON

CENTRAL AFRICAN REPUBLIC

Tuna

Lowland gorilla

EQUATL GUINEA

LIBREVILLE

GABON

Elephant

Pygmy hunters

BRAZZAVILLE

KINSHASA

CABINDA

Matadi

Oil

Oil

Mackerel

LUANDA

Coffee

Benguela

ANGOLA

Millet

Copper

Ovambo houses

Cattle

Lions

Anchovies

Gecko

Pilchards

Bushmen

NAMIBIA

WINDHOEK

Diamonds

Quiver tree

Hake

Orange

SOUTH AFRICA

TABLE MOUNTAIN 1,087 m

Cape Town

Colobus monkey

Crocodile

Ubangi

Zaire (Congo)

Kisangani

Mbandaka

Grey parrot

ZAIRE

Hippopotami

Kasai

Oil palms

Buffalo

Colobus monkey

Diamonds

Hornbill

Diamonds

Rainforest

Cassava

Z

Zambezi

VICTORIA FALLS

Zebra

Springbox

BOTSWANA

KALAHARI DESERT

GABORONE

Oryx

Diamonds

Kimberley

Sheep

SOUTH AFR

Ostriches Port Elizabeth

Wine

CAPE OF GOOD HOPE

ATLANTIC OCEAN

CONGO

SUDAN
ETHIOPIA
SOMALIA

Elephant
Coffee
Giant groundsel
UGANDA
KAMPALA
Cotton
Cheetah
KENYA
Mт KENYA 5,199 m
LAKE TURKANA

Gorilla
KIGALI
RWANDA
BUJUMBURA
BURUNDI
LAKE VICTORIA
GREAT RIFT VALLEY

Chimpanzee
Masai herdsman
NAIROBI
Wildebeest
Coffee
Lions
Mombasa
Tourism
Coconut palms
Dhow

LAKE TANGANYIKA
DODOMA
Mт KILIMANJARO 5,896 m
ZANZIBAR
Dar-es-Salaam

TANZANIA
Tea
Elephants

Copper
ZAMBIA
Leopard
Rhinoceros
Ndola
Copper
MALAWI
GREAT RIFT VALLEY
LAKE NYASA
Crested hornbill
Mangoes

COMOROS
ALDABRA ISLANDS

COMOROS
MAYOTTE (Fr)

LILONGWE
KARIBA DAM
Blantyre
MALAWI
Nacala
Ploughshare tortoise
Vanilla pods

LUSAKA
LAKE KARIBA
Zambezi
MOZAMBIQUE
Tea
Bananas
Lemur
Long-tailed ground roller

ZIMBABWE
HARARE
Soapstone carving
MOZAMBIQUE CHANNEL
ZIMBABWE
ANTANANARIVO
MADAGASCAR

Bulawayo
GREAT ZIMBABWE
Beira
Baobab tree
Black lemur

Limpopo
MOZAMBIQUE
Coelacanth
Chameleon

Gold
Giraffes
Cashew nuts
Octopus tree

PRETORIA
Johannesburg
Zulu
MAPUTO
MBABANE
SWAZI-LAND
Shrimps
SWAZILAND

AFRICA
MASERU
LESOTHO
Durban
Citrus fruits
Tourism
LESOTHO

Umtata
Pineapples
Lobster

INDIAN OCEAN

0 200 400 600 800 Kilometres
0 100 200 300 400 500 Miles

FACTS AND FIGURES

Zebra in the plains of Kenya. In recent years their numbers have been greatly reduced by hunting.

Highest mountains: Mt Kilimanjaro (Tanzania), 5,896 m (19,344 ft); Mt Kenya (Kenya), 5,199 m (17,057 ft).

Longest rivers: Zaire, 4,667 km (2,900 miles); Zambezi, 2,735 km (1,700 miles).

Largest lakes: Lake Victoria, 69,400 sq km (26,800 sq miles); Lake Tanganyika, 32,900 sq km (13,860 sq miles).

Deepest lake: Lake Tanganyika, 1,435 m (4,708 ft).

Largest cities: Kinshasa (Zaire), 2,653,000; Cape Town (South Africa), 1,912,000.

ANGOLA
Capital: Luanda

BOTSWANA
Capital: Gaborone

BURUNDI
Capital: Bujumbura

COMOROS
Capital: Moroni

CONGO
Capital: Brazzaville

EQUATORIAL GUINEA
Capital: Malabo

GABON
Capital: Libreville

KENYA
Capital: Nairobi

LESOTHO
Capital: Maseru

MADAGASCAR
Capital: Antananarivo

MALAWI
Capital: Lilongwe

MOZAMBIQUE
Capital: Maputo

NAMIBIA
Capital: Windhoek

RWANDA
Capital: Kigali

SOUTH AFRICA
National capital: Pretoria
Seat of government: Cape Town

SWAZILAND
Capital: Mbabane

TANZANIA
Capital: Dodoma

UGANDA
Capital: Kampala

ZAIRE
Capital: Kinshasa

ZAMBIA
Capital: Lusaka

ZIMBABWE
Capital: Harare

AUSTRALASIA

AUSTRALASIA is the smallest of the continents and it has fewer people than any other continent except Antarctica. It is named after Australia, the only large piece of land it contains. The continent also covers the islands of New Guinea and New Zealand, and thousands of tiny islands scattered across the Pacific Ocean, many of which are too small to show on the map. Australasia is sometimes referred to as Oceania.

Australia, New Zealand and New Guinea were once joined to the other southern continents, but over millions of years they split off and drifted into the Pacific Ocean. Because Australasia is so isolated, many of the plants and animals which have evolved there are not found anywhere else in the world. The pouched mammals of Australia, such as the kangaroo, wallaby, and koala, and the flightless birds of New Zealand, such as the kiwi and the kakapo, are examples of this.

One of the Fijian islands.

The Pacific islands have been formed in a number of ways. Some of them are the tips of mountains or volcanoes which rise up from the ocean bed. Others are formed of coral, made up of the skeletons of millions of tiny sea creatures.

The Pacific islands fall into three groups, depending on their position in the ocean. In the middle of the Pacific are the Polynesian Islands, of which the biggest are the Hawaiian Islands. By the Stone Age, the light-skinned Polynesian people had become great explorers and navigators. They sailed all over the Pacific in their small double canoes, finding their way from the position of the stars and the patterns of the waves. The Maori people of New Zealand are descended from Polynesians who settled there in about AD 900.

The city of Perth, Australia.

Maori carving, New Zealand.

The Micronesian Islands are situated in the western Pacific. Like the Polynesians, the Micronesians were great seafarers, and traded throughout the region. The dark-skinned Melanesian people live on the islands closest to Australia and are related to the Australian Aborigines. Today, tourism is an important industry in the Pacific islands, and this has brought many changes to the islanders' way of life.

Europeans first began to settle in Australasia in the 18th century. Most of the people who now live in Australia and New Zealand are descendants of settlers from the UK. More recently, immigrants have also come from other parts of Europe, Polynesia, and the Far East.

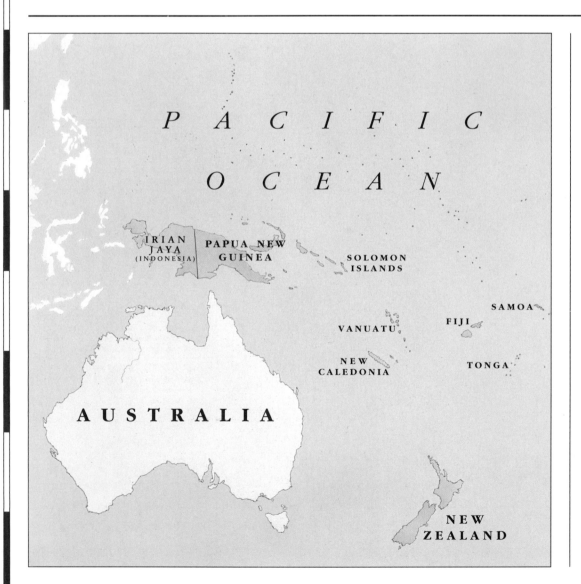

FACTS ABOUT AUSTRALASIA

Area: 8,923,000 sq km (3,445,197 sq miles). Australasia is the smallest of the continents and covers only six per cent of the world's land area.

Population: 25,800,000. Fewer people live in Australasia than any other continent, except Antarctica.

Number of independent countries: 11.

Largest country: Australia, 7,686,848 sq km (2,967,207 sq miles).

Most populated country: Australia, 16,506,000.

Largest cities: Sydney (Australia), 3,531,000; Melbourne (Australia), 2,965,000; Brisbane (Australia), 1,215,000; Perth (Australia), 1,083,000; Adelaide (Australia), 1,013,000; Auckland (New Zealand), 851,000.

Highest mountains: Mt Wilhelm (Papua New Guinea), 4,509 m (14,793 ft); Mt Cook (New Zealand), 3,764 m (12,349 ft); Mt Kosciusko (Australia), 2,228 m (7,310 ft).

Longest river: Murray-Darling (Australia), 3,750 km (2,330 miles).

Largest deserts: Gibson Desert, Great Sandy Desert, Great Victoria Desert, Simpson Desert (all in Australia).

Largest islands: New Guinea, 808,510 sq km (312,168 sq miles); South Island, New Zealand, 150,460 sq km (58,093 sq miles).

Largest lakes: Lake Eyre (Australia), 9,583 sq km (3,700 sq miles); Lake Gairdner (Australia), 7,770 sq km (3,000 sq miles); Lake Torrens (Australia), 5,780 sq km (2,231 sq miles).

Oldest rocks: The oldest rocks ever found on Earth are zircon crystals from the Jack Hills near Perth, Australia. They are 4,300 million years old.

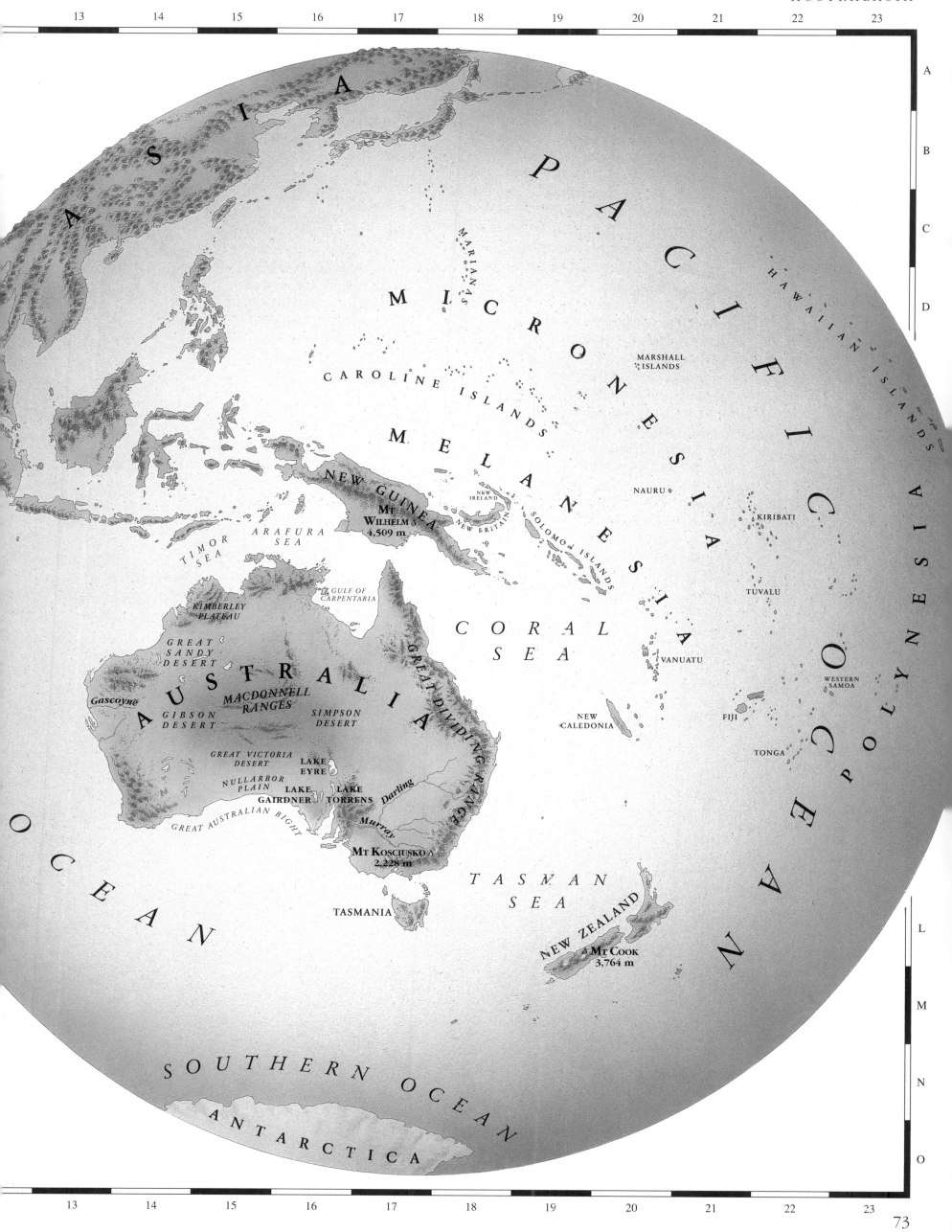

A S I A

P A C I F I C

MARIANAS

HAWAIIAN ISLANDS

M I C R O N E S I A

CAROLINE ISLANDS

MARSHALL
ISLANDS

M E L A N E S I A

NEW GUINEA
Mt
WILHELM
4,509 m

NEW
IRELAND

NEW BRITAIN

SOLOMON ISLANDS

NAURU

KIRIBATI

ARAFURA
SEA

TIMOR
SEA

O C E A N

TUVALU

KIMBERLEY
PLATEAU

GULF OF
CARPENTARIA

C O R A L
S E A

GREAT
SANDY
DESERT

Gascoyne

A U S T R A L I A

MACDONNELL
RANGES

GIBSON
DESERT

SIMPSON
DESERT

VANUATU

WESTERN
SAMOA

GREAT VICTORIA
DESERT

LAKE
EYRE

NULLARBOR
PLAIN

LAKE
GAIRDNER

LAKE
TORRENS

Darling

GREAT DIVIDING RANGE

NEW
CALEDONIA

FIJI

TONGA

P O L Y N E S I A

Murray

GREAT AUSTRALIAN BIGHT

Mt KOSCIUSKO
2,228 m

T A S M A N
S E A

TASMANIA

NEW ZEALAND
Mt COOK
3,764 m

O C E A N

S O U T H E R N   O C E A N

A N T A R C T I C A

1   2   3   4   5   6   7   8   9   10

AUSTRALIA

AUSTRALIA is a country and a continent. It is almost as big as the United States. Much of the country is hot and dry, especially in the middle where there are deserts. Few people live in these dry areas, but there are large sheep and cattle farms called "stations" and some mining. East of the hills and mountains of the Great Dividing Range and on the island of Tasmania the climate is wetter, and it is here that most people live. Two-thirds of all Australians live in the small number of large cities, particularly the state capitals, such as Sydney, Melbourne, and Brisbane. The population of Australia is only 16 million people, compared with 245 million in the United States.

Millions of years ago, Australia drifted away from the other continents of the world. As a result, many of the plants and animals which evolved there are not found anywhere else in the world. Many of the mammals, such as kangaroos and wombats, are marsupials, which rear their young in pouches on their stomachs.

The first inhabitants of Australia were the Aborigines, who arrived about 40,000 years ago. Europeans did not settle in Australia until 200 years ago. Since 1945 the population has doubled, with people coming to Australia from many parts of the world.

THE GREAT BARRIER REEF

The Great Barrier Reef is a maze of about 2,500 coral reefs and islands stretching 2,000 km (1,200 miles) along the coast of Queensland. It contains over 300 different species of coral and thousands of fish. Coral is formed by millions of tiny sea animals called polyps, which cement themselves together. The Great Barrier Reef is slowly being eaten away by creatures called crown-of-thorns starfish. In order to protect the reef from further destruction by both humans and natural causes, the Great Barrier Reef Marine Park has been formed.

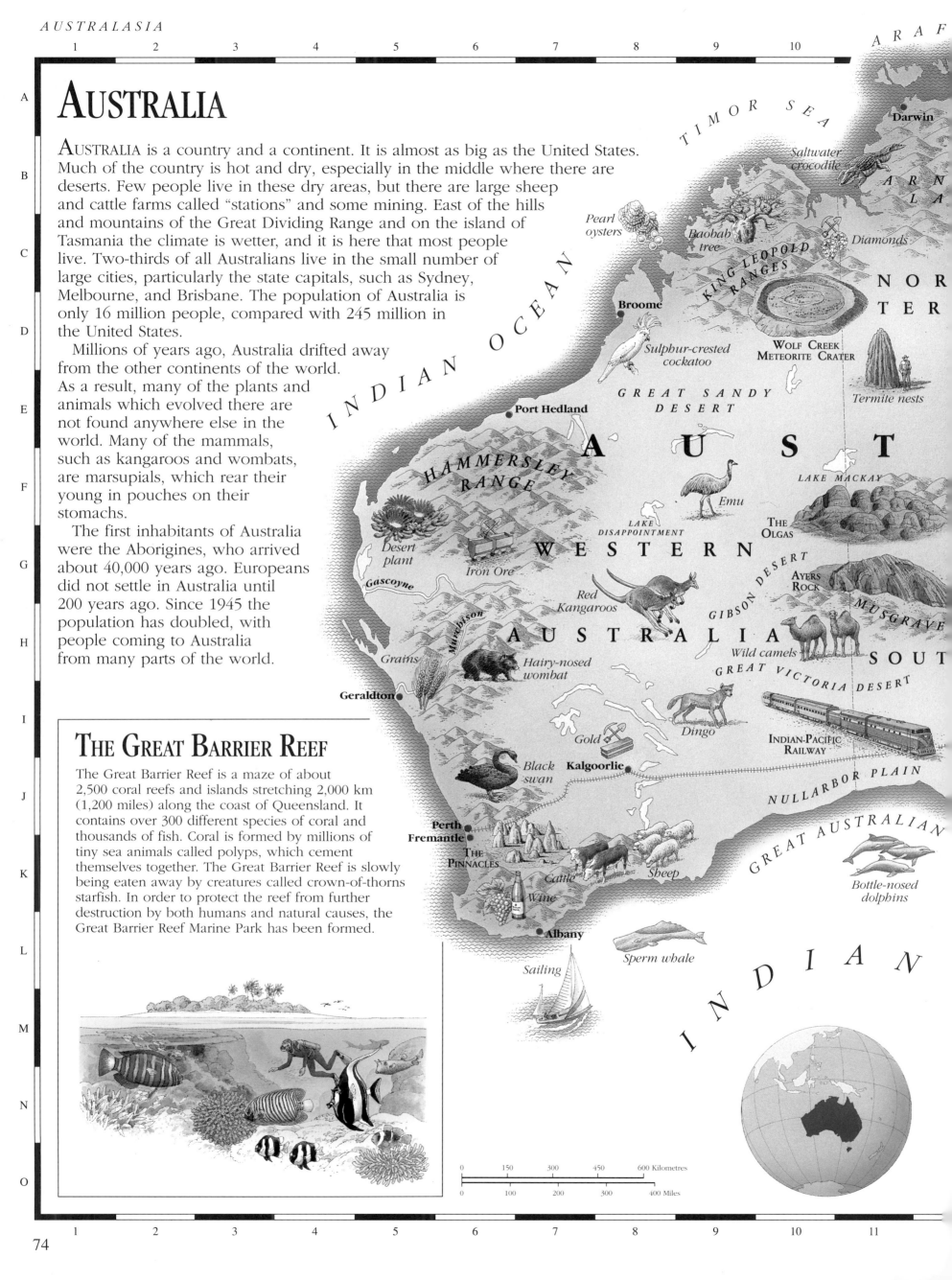

TIMOR SEA

ARAF

Darwin

Saltwater crocodile

ARNL A

Pearl oysters

Baobab tree

Diamonds

KING LEOPOLD RANGES

NOR TER

Broome

Sulphur-crested cockatoo

WOLF CREEK METEORITE CRATER

INDIAN OCEAN

Termite nests

Port Hedland

GREAT SANDY DESERT

AUST

HAMMERSLEY RANGE

Emu

LAKE MACKAY

Desert plant

LAKE DISAPPOINTMENT

THE OLGAS

WESTERN

Iron Ore

GIBSON DESERT

AYERS ROCK

Gascoyne

Red Kangaroos

MUSGRAVE

AUSTRALIA

SOUT

Grains

Hairy-nosed wombat

Wild camels

GREAT VICTORIA DESERT

Geraldton

Dingo

INDIAN-PACIFIC RAILWAY

Gold

Black swan

Kalgoorlie

NULLARBOR PLAIN

Perth
Fremantle

THE PINNACLES

Cattle

Sheep

GREAT AUSTRALIAN

Wine

Bottle-nosed dolphins

Albany

Sperm whale

INDIAN

Sailing

0   150   300   450   600 Kilometres

0   100   200   300   400 Miles

1   2   3   4   5   6   7   8   9   10   11

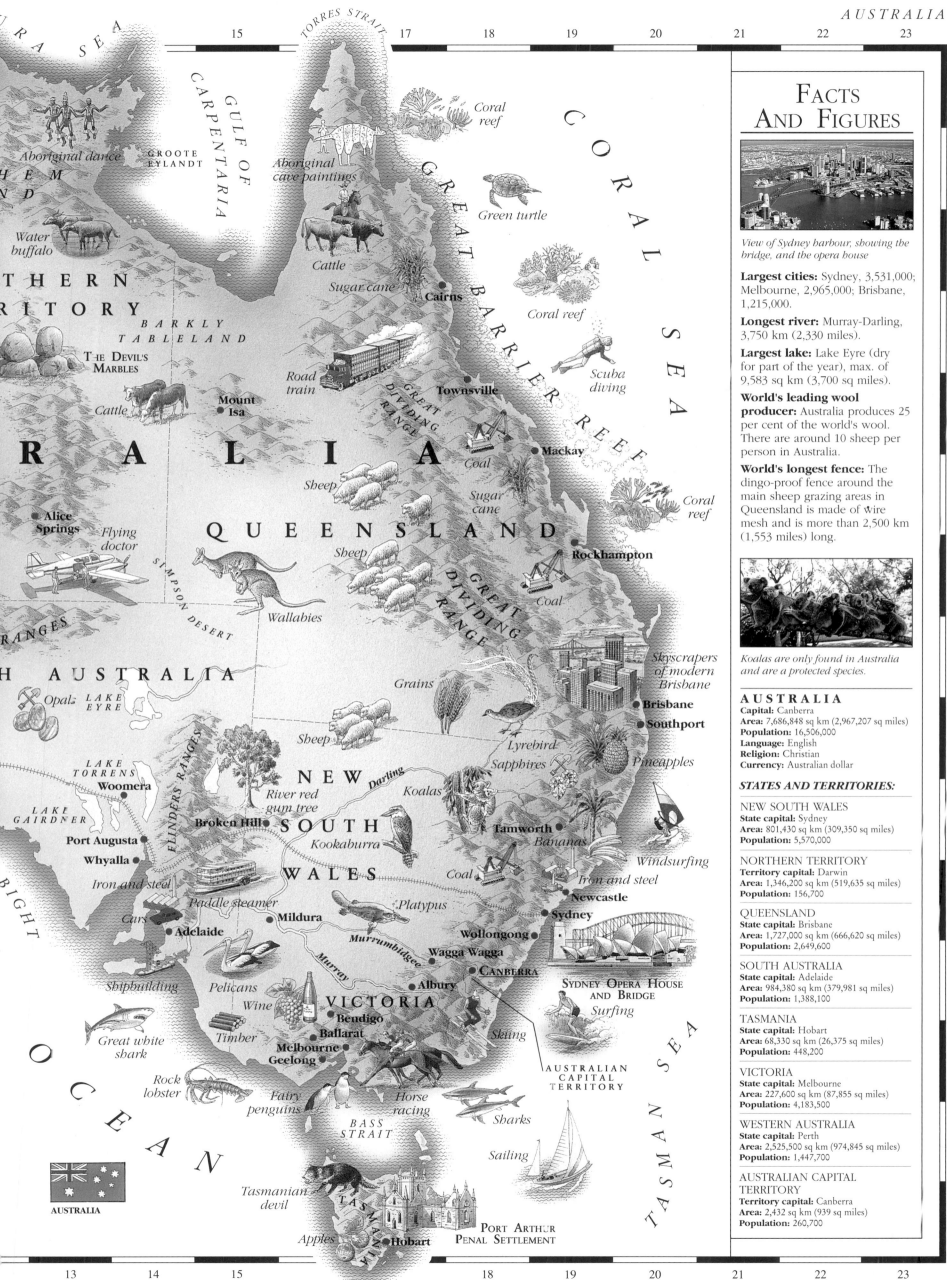

A U R A   S E A

TORRES STRAIT

GULF OF CARPENTARIA

Aboriginal dance

GROOTE EYLANDT

Water buffalo

HEM ND

THERN RITORY

Aboriginal cave paintings

Coral reef

C O R A L   S E A

Green turtle

Scuba diving

Coral reef

GREAT BARRIER REEF

Cattle

Sugar cane

● **Cairns**

BARKLY TABLELAND

THE DEVIL'S MARBLES

Cattle

● **Mount Isa**

Road train

Townsville ●

GREAT DIVIDING RANGE

Coal

● **Mackay**

R A L I A

Sheep

Sugar cane

Coral reef

● **Alice Springs**

Flying doctor

Q U E E N S L A N D

Sheep

Rockhampton ●

Coal

SIMPSON DESERT

Wallabies

GREAT DIVIDING RANGE

RANGES

H   A U S T R A L I A

Opal LAKE EYRE

Grains

Skyscrapers of modern Brisbane

Brisbane

Southport

Sheep

Lyrebird

Sapphires

Pineapples

LAKE TORRENS

FLINDERS RANGES

River red gum tree

N E W

Darling

Koalas

Woomera

Broken Hill ●

S O U T H

Sheep

Kookaburra

● **Tamworth**

Bananas

LAKE GAIRDNER

Port Augusta

Whyalla

W A L E S

Coal

Iron and steel

Iron and steel

Paddle steamer

Newcastle ●

Cars

Platypus

● **Sydney**

Mildura ●

Murrumbidgee

● **Adelaide**

Pelicans

Murray

Wollongong

Wagga Wagga ●

Shipbuilding

Pelicans

Wine

CANBERRA

● **Albury**

B I G H T

Great white shark

Timber

V I C T O R I A

Bendigo ●

Ballarat ●

Skiing

SYDNEY OPERA HOUSE AND BRIDGE

Surfing

Windsurfing

Rock lobster

Melbourne ●
Geelong ●

Horse racing

Sharks

AUSTRALIAN CAPITAL TERRITORY

O C E A N

Fairy penguins

BASS STRAIT

Sailing

T A S M A N   S E A

AUSTRALIA

Tasmanian devil

T A S M A N

PORT ARTHUR PENAL SETTLEMENT

Apples

● **Hobart**

FACTS AND FIGURES

View of Sydney harbour, showing the bridge, and the opera house

Largest cities: Sydney, 3,531,000; Melbourne, 2,965,000; Brisbane, 1,215,000.

Longest river: Murray-Darling, 3,750 km (2,330 miles).

Largest lake: Lake Eyre (dry for part of the year), max. of 9,583 sq km (3,700 sq miles).

World's leading wool producer: Australia produces 25 per cent of the world's wool. There are around 10 sheep per person in Australia.

World's longest fence: The dingo-proof fence around the main sheep grazing areas in Queensland is made of wire mesh and is more than 2,500 km (1,553 miles) long.

Koalas are only found in Australia and are a protected species.

AUSTRALIA
Capital: Canberra
Area: 7,686,848 sq km (2,967,207 sq miles)
Population: 16,506,000
Language: English
Religion: Christian
Currency: Australian dollar

STATES AND TERRITORIES:

NEW SOUTH WALES
State capital: Sydney
Area: 801,430 sq km (309,350 sq miles)
Population: 5,570,000

NORTHERN TERRITORY
Territory capital: Darwin
Area: 1,346,200 sq km (519,635 sq miles)
Population: 156,700

QUEENSLAND
State capital: Brisbane
Area: 1,727,000 sq km (666,620 sq miles)
Population: 2,649,600

SOUTH AUSTRALIA
State capital: Adelaide
Area: 984,380 sq km (379,981 sq miles)
Population: 1,388,100

TASMANIA
State capital: Hobart
Area: 68,330 sq km (26,375 sq miles)
Population: 448,200

VICTORIA
State capital: Melbourne
Area: 227,600 sq km (87,855 sq miles)
Population: 4,183,500

WESTERN AUSTRALIA
State capital: Perth
Area: 2,525,500 sq km (974,845 sq miles)
Population: 1,447,700

AUSTRALIAN CAPITAL TERRITORY
Territory capital: Canberra
Area: 2,432 sq km (939 sq miles)
Population: 260,700

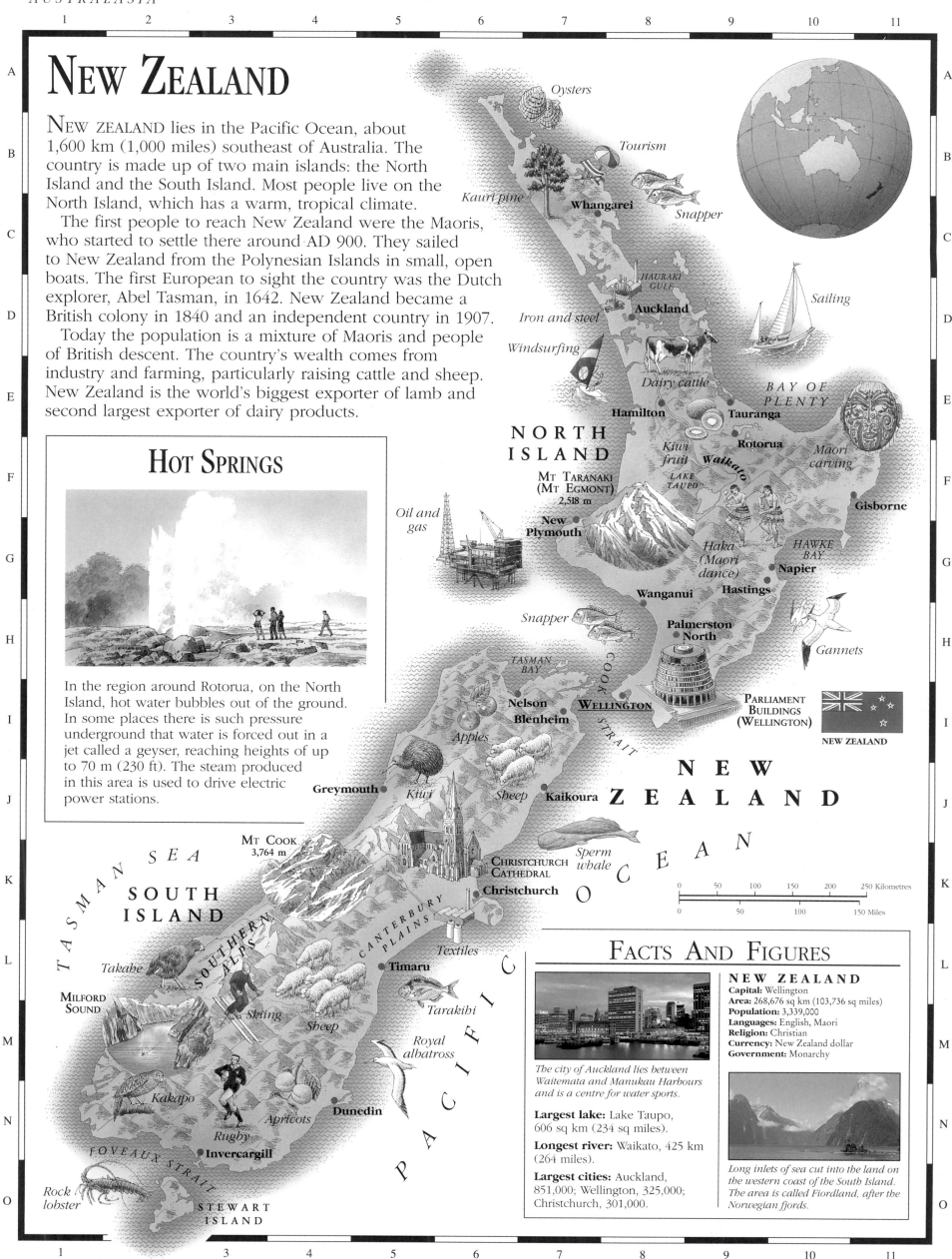

NEW ZEALAND

NEW ZEALAND lies in the Pacific Ocean, about 1,600 km (1,000 miles) southeast of Australia. The country is made up of two main islands: the North Island and the South Island. Most people live on the North Island, which has a warm, tropical climate.

The first people to reach New Zealand were the Maoris, who started to settle there around AD 900. They sailed to New Zealand from the Polynesian Islands in small, open boats. The first European to sight the country was the Dutch explorer, Abel Tasman, in 1642. New Zealand became a British colony in 1840 and an independent country in 1907.

Today the population is a mixture of Maoris and people of British descent. The country's wealth comes from industry and farming, particularly raising cattle and sheep. New Zealand is the world's biggest exporter of lamb and second largest exporter of dairy products.

HOT SPRINGS

In the region around Rotorua, on the North Island, hot water bubbles out of the ground. In some places there is such pressure underground that water is forced out in a jet called a geyser, reaching heights of up to 70 m (230 ft). The steam produced in this area is used to drive electric power stations.

Oysters
Tourism
Kauri pine
Whangarei
Snapper
HAURAKI GULF
Auckland
Sailing
Iron and steel
Windsurfing
Dairy cattle
BAY OF PLENTY

NORTH ISLAND
Hamilton
Tauranga
Kiwi fruit
Rotorua
Maori carving
Waikato
MT TARANAKI (MT EGMONT) 2,518 m
LAKE TAUPO
Oil and gas
New Plymouth
Haka (Maori dance)
HAWKE BAY
Gisborne
Napier
Wanganui
Hastings
Snapper
Palmerston North
Gannets
TASMAN BAY
Nelson
Blenheim
Apples
COOK STRAIT
WELLINGTON
PARLIAMENT BUILDINGS (WELLINGTON)

NEW ZEALAND

NEW ZEALAND

Greymouth
Kiwi
Sheep
Kaikoura
Sperm whale
MT COOK 3,764 m
CHRISTCHURCH CATHEDRAL
Christchurch

TASMAN SEA
SOUTH ISLAND
SOUTHERN ALPS
CANTERBURY PLAINS
Textiles
Takahe
Skiing
Sheep
Timaru
MILFORD SOUND
Tarakihi
Royal albatross
Kakapo
Apricots
Dunedin
Rugby
Invercargill
FOVEAUX STRAIT
Rock lobster
STEWART ISLAND
PACIFIC OCEAN

FACTS AND FIGURES

The city of Auckland lies between Waitemata and Manukau Harbours and is a centre for water sports.

NEW ZEALAND
Capital: Wellington
Area: 268,676 sq km (103,736 sq miles)
Population: 3,339,000
Languages: English, Maori
Religion: Christian
Currency: New Zealand dollar
Government: Monarchy

Largest lake: Lake Taupo, 606 sq km (234 sq miles).

Longest river: Waikato, 425 km (264 miles).

Largest cities: Auckland, 851,000; Wellington, 325,000; Christchurch, 301,000.

Long inlets of sea cut into the land on the western coast of the South Island. The area is called Fiordland, after the Norwegian fjords.

INDEX

This index contains the names of places shown on continental and country maps.
The page number is given in bold type after the place name. The grid reference
follows in lighter type (see also page 13, How to Use This Atlas).

ACKNOWLEDGMENTS

Dorling Kindersley would like to thank the following:
Kate Woodward and Anna Kunst for research, Chris Scollen and Richard Czapnik for additional design help, and Struan Reid for editorial assistance.

Picture Research Cynthia Hole

Political Maps Luciano Corbella

Picture credits
(r = right, l = left, t = top, c = centre, b = bottom)

Australian Overseas Information Service, London 75tr, 75br
Australian Tourist Commission, London 72tr

de Beers 66tr
Charles Bowman 16br, 25tr, 34c, 51tr, 51tl, 52tl, 59tr, 59br, 76tl,
Canadian High Commission 16tc, 19tc
Caribbean Tourist Office 27tr
The J. Allan Cash Photolibrary 6tr, 6bl, 12tl, 12br, 20tr, 23br, 23bl, 36tl, 36br, 45tl, 76br,
Lester Cheeseman 52bc, 65tl, 65bc, 66tr
Chilean Embassy 33br, 33bl
Chinese Tourist Office 63br
Bruce Coleman Ltd / Fritz Prenzel 7cl,
Commission of the European Communities 34tl
Susan Cunningham 31br
Richard Czapnik 66c
Egyptian Tourist Office 57tr, 69tl

Chris Fairclough Colour Library 12c, 21tr, 43tr, 43br, 45c, 52tr, 72c, 72bl,
Fiat Press Office 46cr
French Railways Ltd 39cr
Susan Griggs Agency / Rob Cousins 7tl; George Hall 12tr
Robert Harding Picture Library 6tl
Hutchison Library / John Dowman 6br; Anwa Tully 12bl
The Image Bank / Guido Rossi 12bc
Italian State Tourist Office 46tl
Kenyan Tourist Office 71tr
Anna Kunst 55tr, 55cr
Keith Lye 16cl, 28tl, 28bc, 52tr, 57br, 63tr
Hugo Maertens 41br

Norwegian Tourist Office 14tr, 15tr
Peruvian Embassy 28tr, 31tr
Roger Priddy 34tr, 36tr, 39tr, 39br, 46cl
South American Pictures 33tl
Spanish National Tourist Office 49tr
The Telegraph Colour Library 41bl
Travel Photo International 7tr, 7cr, 41tr, 43cr, 45br, 49br
Zefa Picture Library 12cr
Zentrale Farbbild Agentur / D. Fröbisch 7br

Every effort has been made to trace the copyright holders and we apologise in advance for any unintentional omissions. We would be pleased to insert the appropriate acknowledgment in any subsequent edition of this book.